JUDICIAL DISCRETION AND THE RIGHT TO PROPERTY

SATVINDER S. JUSS

With a Foreword by
The Hon. Sir Gavin Lightman

PINTER

London and Washington

CITIZENSHIP AND THE LAW SERIES

General Editor
ROBERT BLACKBURN
Professor of Constitutional Law,
King's College, University of London

For my Rani
— forever constant

First published 1998 by
Pinter, A Cassell Imprint
Wellington House, 125 Strand, London WC2R 0BB, England
PO Box 605, Herndon, Virginia 20172, USA

British Library Cataloguing in Publication Data
A catalogue record for this book is available from the British Library

ISBN 1-85567-531-5

Typeset by York House Typographic Ltd, London
Printed and bound in Great Britain by
Bookcraft (Bath) Ltd, Midsomer Norton, Somerset

Contents

Foreword

The law in any society reflects the social and other values in that society, and the law must adapt as those values change. The role of making those adaptations in the United Kingdom is shared between the legislature and the courts. The doctrines of the separation of powers and of the supremacy of Parliament render legislative action the preferred and often the only option, but the pivotal role of the judges arises from the lack of Parliamentary will, attention and time and the constitutional duty of the courts to construe legislation.

In the field of statutory construction, the judges recognize that legislation is the prerogative of Parliament, and accordingly the role of the court should be 'purposive' rather than 'creative'.[1] That is to say, the courts should seek to elicit from the legislation and its history the purpose (social or otherwise) which Parliament intended to achieve and, in its construction of the legislation, seek to effectuate that intention, and not substitute its own. But in the field of case law (known generally as the Common Law), since this is the creation of the judges, the judges are freer (indeed duty-bound) to restate the principles so that they accord with current conditions and needs. In practice the difference between these two approaches is not always great or indeed perceptible, for the intention to be imputed to Parliament (where this is possible) is likely to reflect the value judgments of the judiciary.[2]

The view may fairly be taken that the primary preoccupation of English law until the eighteenth century was with property rights; that the eighteenth century was a period of concern with civil rights; that the nineteenth century has been concerned with social rights (see pp. 55ff.). It is today explicitly accepted that questions of social justice, and how best to achieve it, are inherent in the judicial process.[3] Judges have a civic resposibility (so far as is practicable) to develop a socially just system of law. In a caring and just society all citizens must have a sense of belonging: grounds for a sense of alienation on the part of any section or group (which is a prime cause of divisiveness in society and social breakdown) must (so far as possible) be eliminated. To achieve this goal there is a need to identify and afford recognition to those rights and values which are indispensable to the existence and preservation of the fabric of a stable community. These include the essential requirements for the life, human dignity and self-respect of its citizens and most particularly those who are on the margins of society. The courts (like society as a whole) are increasingly sensitive to these considerations. The courts should receive a substantial further impetus in this direction once the Human Rights Bill has passed into law. For the Bill will afford statutory recognition and reinforcement to those fundamental human rights, and this should colour, if not directly influence, judicial thinking and legal developments in every area of law.

The field of property law has seen the conscience of the courts struggle to protect the essential need to a roof over the heads of those especially vulnerable and at risk. In the 1950s Lord Denning invented an 'equity' to protect deserted wives from being evicted from their homes,[4] but this proved too much and too bold for the House of Lords to sanction.[5] Parliament had to intervene to provide equivalent statutory protection.[6] The House of Lords however later proved creative in protecting the interests of partners who contributed to the purchase of a home;[7] in setting aside security interests granted by them under undue influence;[8] and in preventing a landlord (by exercise of superior bargaining power over the homeless) from reducing the status of the interest granted from that of a (Rent Act-protected) tenancy to that of a licence by the expedient of attaching to the grant the label of a licence.[9]

Dr Satvinder Juss in this work has conducted an in-depth analysis of the authorities and developments in this field of law. His thesis is that the law should go much further: that the wealth of individuals and institutions should be treated as held on a 'social trust' to confer social benefits, and that property rights should be subordinated to personal rights (e.g., to human security) in order to achieve a more egalitarian society.

His work is invaluable, not merely as a historical study, but as a source and inspiration for further research in other fields of law and for the future development of the law to meet the demands made of it in a socially just society. Dr Juss's views are forthright, challenging and controversial. It is possible to disagree with them, but they cannot be ignored.

SIR GAVIN LIGHTMAN
Royal Courts of Justice
London

Notes

1 Consider the speech of Lord Lloyd in *Investors Compensation Schemes Limited* v. *West Bromwich Building Society* [1998] 1 All ER 98 at 106.

2 See, e.g., *Antoniades* v. *Villiers* [1995] 1 AC 417.

3 See, e.g., Lord Scarman in *Williams & Glyn's Bank* v. *Boland* [1981] AC 487 at 510.

4 See *National Provincial Bank* v. *Ainsworth* [1964] Ch 665 and cases cited.

5 See *National Provincial Bank* v. *Ainsworth* [1965] AC 1175.

6 Matrimonial Homes Act 1967, later replaced by the Matrimonial Homes Act 1983.

7 See *Williams & Glyn's Bank* v. *Boland* [1981] AC 487.

8 See *Barclays Bank* v. *O'Brien* [1994] AC 140.

9 See *Street* v. *Mountford* [1985] AC 809. The Court of Appeal has very recently placed a gloss on this decision, so as to enable a housing trust, itself a licensee of a local authority, to perform the socially valuable function of providing exclusive possession of accommodation to the homeless by way of the grant of a licence instead of the grant of a tenancy: see *Bruton* v. *London Housing Trust* [1997] 4 AER 970 in effect overruling its earlier decision in *Housing Association* v. *Jones* [1990] 1 WLR 779.

Preface

Proputty, proputty, proputty, proputty
That's what the judges and historians say.
Tennyson

Few books on property law recognize the importance of judicial discretion. Few, the importance of judicial value. Yet these are critical to the protection of property rights in society. Judges make powerful value preferences when applying the law to individual cases. When cases are hard there is simply no such thing as just applying the law. Yet judges have not infrequently maintained the fiction that there is. Harold Laski once suffered an unexpected rebuke from Mr Justice MacNaghten of the High Court when he had the temerity to inform him that in hard cases, judges must 'exercise the sovereign prerogative of choice' and make law. In a letter to Justice Oliver Wendell Holmes of the US Supreme Court in 1932, a bruised Laski recalls that MacNaghten told him that 'he simply applied the law, looking neither to the right nor to the left' and that 'no damned nonsense' was going to get him to change his judicial conduct.

Today, sophisticated judges take a more measured approach to judicial decision-making, though the answers to a proper judicial approach are none the clearer. In 1972, Lord Reid admitted that grown-up lawyers have ceased to believe in the 'fairy-tale' that 'in some Aladdin's Cave' is the hidden key to correct judicial interpretation. Yet a discreet and flexible approach is crucial to the proper determination of important rights of human dignity, such as property rights, in an ever more complex society of our times.

Property rights are the bed-rock of our traditional system of common law. If there is one area of the law which has been shored up by both judges and Parliament, it is the right to property. There are, after all, no property rights in the abstract, save what the law, through its established institutions, decrees. As Jeremy Bentham observed in the nineteenth century in his *Principles of the Civil Code of Property*, all too well,

> we shall see that there is no natural property – that property is entirely the creature of law. . . . the idea of property consists in an established expectation – in the persuasion of the power to derive certain advantages from the object, according to the nature of the case. But this expectation, this persuasion, can only be the work of the law.[1]

Judges are central players in determining rights of property in courts of law through the exercise of individual discretionary choices.

There has been little discussion of the role of judges in ascribing property rights.[2] There has been even less discussion of what values they seek to promote, or should be seen to be promoting. However, an analysis of judicial decision-making in property disputes would be timely. The theories of property rights have, after all, been well discussed in most philosophical treatments of property. A critical account of the traditional theories took place most notably as long ago as 1934 in Harold Laski's classic *A Grammar of Politics*.[3] In modern Anglo-American theory the concept of property has most famously been discussed by Charles Reich in his 1964 article 'The new property', easily becoming the most frequently quoted article from the *Yale Law Journal*, and bringing in its wake much impassioned commentary and criticism.[4] Recently, J. W. Harris, in bringing together the various philosophical discourses on this subject, in his excellent *Property and Justice*, has asked a question that even decision-makers in courts of law – inasmuch as they are concerned with the ideal of justice – should bring within their contemplation. Harris asks:

> suppose we agree, minimally, that justice makes the following demands: people should not be treated differently on the basis that some kinds of human beings are inherently inferior to others; some degree of autonomous choice should be accorded to everyone; and unprovoked invasions of bodily integrity should be banned. Does it follow that the external resources of the world ought to be brought within the domain of some kind of property institution?[5]

In the impeccable analysis that follows, Harris considers possible answers to this question, and includes a chapter on the 'Instrumental Values of Property',[6] a discussion of values that is no doubt of relevance to judicial decision-making as well.

The object of this book, however, is more mundane but, it is hoped, no less important. After suggesting that values are central to how property rights can be fashioned in a morally satisfying and ethically coherent manner, this work considers three of the most contentious areas of property law adjudication in recent English land law. It undertakes a case by case analysis of individual judicial pronouncements in these three areas and suggests that decision-makers are often not engaged in a dispassionate rule and rote application of statutory law, but are rather making choices with a view to doing justice as they see it. The question then is, how can the judicial function best be performed? And what values can be best enhanced?

In this book, it is suggested that the exercise of discretion in the courts should respect and promote integrity in the law. By this we mean that laws regarding property rights must be staked out on more clear and morally defensible grounds than they presently are. They should ensure social justice in the community because this is the cardinal public value in liberal societies based on equal citizenship rights for all. Today citizenship rights are important for a moral framework of rights and for the development of an idea of moral property. Property rights are immoral if they do not take into account the inequality of personal bargaining power in addressing a person's basic individual needs. Citizenship is an important concept through which to structure the exercise of judicial discretion when it bears on personal property rights. Citizenship is a central concept for the person in liberal democratic societies. It is also the most important political problem that faces post-welfare societies like Britain today at the end of the twentieth century. Citizenship today has to be given a contemporary meaning that is more personal. The concept of citizenship should be used to integrate the individual poor, the oppressed, the dispossessed, the racial minorities and all those that exist on the fringes of society into the mainstream of community life. It should accord them full membership rights and a sense of belonging within the state. The writer has considered this question not only in relation to those within the community, such as here with respect to property rights, but also, in an earlier work, in relation to those without the community, with respect to immigrant rights,[7] and has analysed how the exercise of discretion by decision-makers can have an impact on the development of community rights.

It is suggested here that the masterly analysis of T. H. Marshall on citizenship should be used as a base. Nearly half a century ago he wrote *Citizenship and Social Class*. He argued that citizenship is not just a basic matter of political status in the community, but that it implies equal civil, political and social rights and duties. This analysis should be used as a springboard from which to develop a moral idea of property rights that are based on a real sense of communal citizenship at a personal level. It is suggested that, as a contemporary idea, citizenship implies an acceptance of the egalitarian social contract. This requires decision-makers to apply principles of parity and equity. These values would be achievable by judges encouraging a reliance on social facts and statistics in the form of a 'Brandeis Brief' (see p. 64) while giving short shrift to legal citations. In relation to possession proceedings, this would mean, for example, that the courts can properly and validly bring themselves to speak to the high rates of possession proceedings in the late 1980s and the early 1990s and their deleterious effects on property, economy, and the person.

The chapters in this book show that the courts can legitimately perform this role and use social data more determinedly. Thus, after a brief discussion in Chapter 1 of the development of an idea of moral property, Chapter 2 deals with the consequence of a bank or building society mortgage charges being taken over a family home, by one co-owner partner at the instance of the other, in circumstances that are not evident to outsiders. This kind of case involving manipulated partners who had been subjected to misrepresentation, duress, undue influence, or unconscionable bargains reached its high water mark in the *O'Brien* case in 1993. Despite the clarification of principle in that case, cases subsequent to *O'Brien* did not always live up to the principles in that case. However, in the *Banco Exterior* case Hobhouse LJ, in an activist approach that upheld the egalitarian social contract, held that it must be entirely within the contemplation of the bank that the wife would come under the undue pressure of her husband. The solicitor therefore, properly exercising his role, should have said to the wife 'You do have a choice and I must advise you that it is not in your best interests to sign this document. You should feel under no obligation to do so. My advice to you is: do not sign.'

In Chapter 3 there is discussion of bankruptcy cases with a trustee in bankruptcy requesting the court to sell the family home for the benefit of creditors with the resultant eviction of the family from the home. Bankruptcy case law is a fertile area in which to study the application of citizenship values. Despite the fact that the exercise of the Section 30 discretion under the Law of Property Act has invariably led to eviction being granted at the behest of a trustee in bankruptcy, the egalitarian social contract has been upheld by individual judges. Bingham LJ, in *In re Citro*, held that a simple balance between the interests of the creditors against those of the wife, with the interest of the creditors simply being one element in the scales, would be 'conducive to justice in the broadest sense and it reflects the preference which the law increasingly gives to personal over property interests'. This is despite the fact that Nourse LJ, in assessing 'exceptional circumstances' in the same case, had taken the view that 'it is not uncommon for a wife with young children to be faced with eviction in circumstances where the realisation of the beneficial interest will not produce enough to buy a comparable home' and 'such circumstances, while engendering a natural sympathy in all who hear of them, cannot be described as exceptional'. Both judgments, it is respectfully submitted, are perfectly persuasive in law. Yet, they demonstrate the impact of different values in the judicial process. One looks to justice for the creditors; the other looks to equity and parity for the wife.

In the final chapter, we look to the importance of residential security in the context of the well-known leases/licences debate. In this context, if one is to evaluate the importance of the egalitarian social contract, one can do no better than quote from the judgment of Lord Templeman in *Street* and *Mountford* when he recognized the lack of parity and equity in the housing market by saying that 'Parties to an agreement cannot contract out of the Rent Acts; if they were to do so the Acts would be a dead letter because in a state of housing shortage a person seeking residential accommodation may agree to anything to obtain shelter'.

Thanks are due to Sir Gavin Lightman for his sparkling foreword and to the author's wife, Rani, for her love and support. The author is also grateful for the year spent in the US with his wife as a Harkness Fellow working in Washington DC and at Harvard Law School, where he also held a Human Rights Fellowship. He is grateful also for his time as Visiting Scholar at the Georgetown Law Center and as a Foreign Visiting Scholar at the Federal Judicial Center in Washington DC and for the generosity of all whom he met during that same period.

SATVINDER S. JUSS
Human Rights Programme
Harvard Law School
Boston

Notes and References

1 Bentham, Jeremy (1859) *Principles of the Civil Code*, ch. 8 (ed. Bowring). London.
2 A notable exception is Gray, Kevin (1993) *Elements of Land Law* (2nd edn) *passim*. London.
3 Laski, Harold J. (1934) *A Grammar of Politics*, ch. 5 (3rd edn). London.
4 Reich, Charles (1964) The new property. *Yale Law Journal* (73), p. 733.
5 Harris, J. W. (1996) *Property and Justice*, p. viii. Oxford.
6 *Ibid.*, ch. 15, pp. 278–307.
7 See Juss, Satvinder (1997) *Discretion and Deviation in the Administration of Immigration Control*. London.

Table of Cases

Table of Statutes

1

Towards an Idea of Moral Property

The reason why men enter into society is the preservation of their property – *John Locke*

If the role of the modern liberal state is to protect the rights of individuals, then among the most important of such rights is the right to property. Private property is the basis of liberty. Even democracy is said to be dependent on the right to private property. According to Professor Milton Friedman, the only places where liberal democracy flourishes are countries with capitalist economies, so that the modern conception of liberty is ultimately dependent upon property.[1] However, if liberty is synonymous with private property it is only because the present tradition of liberalism stands for non-interference. Here ownership of property is seen as control of resources which any individual can exercise without interference from others.[2] This study does not focus on this majoritarian idea of liberty, but rather it concerns itself with the liberty of the weak as well as that of the strong in society on the basis of the equal moral worth of all individuals who are equally deserving of protection by the state.[3]

This begs the question: Can property form the basis of integrity? What do we mean by integrity? Before we answer this question we must remember that posing this question presents a dilemma for property lawyers. For instance, the reason why the right to property is not constitutionally guaranteed is that it is controversial on account of the inequalities in society and the finite economic resources. Where such a right is guaranteed it is often weak, safeguarding the right of the individual against the state, rather than the right of one individual as against the other. Thus, the European Convention on Human Rights 1950 only protects this right under its first protocol. Here Article 1, first, recognizes the general right to property; second, it declares that the individual deprivation of property may only be undertaken in the public interest and subject to certain conditions; and third, it affirms the principle that while the state is not absolutely free to deprive people of their property, it nonetheless has the right to control the use of property rights in the general interest. When we say that property rights must respect integrity, we mean that the laws respecting property must be staked out on more clear and morally defensible grounds that seek to attain social justice, because this is what we expect of our law-makers in liberal societies based on equal citizenship rights for all. If this is so, we need to define such concepts as liberty, property, social justice and citizenship rights. Let us first look at liberty. In the ensuing analysis, liberty is taken to mean essentially social liberty.

Moral Basis of Property Rights

In a moral framework of rights, the right to social liberty would be part of the individual right to self-respect. Self-respect is important in free societies. It is the basis for the expression of a developed personality. Liberty needs to be socially located with its moral convictions, because moral boundaries are important to a fulfilling social existence. Social liberty would then embrace all the personal rights that we regard as being basic and sacrosanct, such as the right to personal security, the right to education, and the right to religious toleration, because all of us want each of these things in free societies. Thus defined, liberty would not be dependent upon strident self-assertion of only some members of society, who are able to avail themselves of freedom of contract at the expense of others, with unequal bargaining power in a common-law legal system, because they threaten to rob others of what others, who are less fortunate, need. Indeed, those who have seen liberty in this way have, in the past, been criticized by R. A. Tawney.[4] They have in modern times been challenged by John Rawls in *A Theory of Justice*. Rawls has referred to certain welfare orientated indispensable rights as being the 'primary goods'.[5] These rights are surely critical to social liberty. Primary goods are goods which enable us all to make something of our lives. With these constraints, and defined in this way, the right to property can be seen as an aid to widespread self-fulfilment[6] in a social sense and not as a means of profiteering as an end in itself. If property can be viewed in this way, then the idea of liberty can be socially located. Within a common-law tradition, social rights have often assumed an importance secondary to economic rights.

Yet economic liberties cannot be divorced from other liberties. The right to property may for individuals be both an economic right or a social right. But which one is to be preferred? We know they are indivisible because, in fact, they are interdependent and interlinked. We need, therefore, to find a way of looking at property and people that does not use a language of exclusionary rights, but something more transcendant. As Justice Stewart observed in the American case of *Lynch* v. *Household Finance Corporation* (1972), 'the dichotomy between personal liberties and property rights is a false one. Property does not have rights. People have rights. ... In fact, a fundamental interdependence exists between the personal right to liberty and the personal right in property. Neither could have meaning without the other. That rights in property are basic civil rights has long been recognised ...'[7] This clearly suggests that there is an analytic weakness in the distinction between economic and non-economic rights. Further, the distinction also overlooks the importance of property and contract in protecting, not only the possessed, but also the dispossessed. What is needed is a conception of property rights that is morally defensible. This can be found in the idea of legal integrity.

If the rights to bodily integrity are one of the 'primary goods' in life then the right to dignity, self-respect, fulfilment and minimal subsistence is also one of the 'primary rights' that give rise to affirmative governmental duties for which there should be a judicially cognizable remedy. This is what we mean by integrity in the law, where both the people concerned and the legal rules that affect them are involved in developmental relationship of evolution and synthesis. The laws are both internally consistent within themselves and externally consistent with those whom they affect. This book sets out to examine how, if at all, a judicially cognizable remedy is provided by the courts in cases of such need for the poor and the dispossessed. In so doing, this work examines the way in which the courts exercise their discretion in relation to property matters and asks if judicial discretion cannot be better exercised to meet the needs of modern contemporary liberal societies today. Before considering judicial discretion, we must define property. This we do next.

Property as a Basis for Social Liberty

Before we can decide what values decision-makers need to promote we need to be sure what property rights are at stake. This is a difficult task because the right to property cannot be pinpointed with the same exactitude as the right, for example, to life, liberty and security. Life, liberty and security follow squarely within the liberal tradition. They are rights because they can be safeguarded by imposing a negative duty on others not to interfere with the sanctity of the person. The same cannot be said about the right to property.[8]

Property is mostly in a person a positive right because it implies the right to ownership by that person. 'Ownership comprises the right to possess', as A. M. Honore has explained, 'the right to use, the right to manage, the right to the income of the thing, the right to the capital, the right to security, the rights of incidents of transmissibility and the absence of term, the prohibition of harmful use, liability to execution, and the incident of residuarity.'[9] These are mostly rights that are acquired in some positive way. They cannot be characterized as rights of non-interference. Yet may not the 'right to security', as Honore says, form the basis to a very definite right to property in a free and liberal society? May it not be the central basis in the concept of legal integrity that incorporates social and communitarian rights?

Suppose that, in a well-known case like *Bull* v. *Bull*,[10] a mother conveys the legal title of a dwelling house in which she has a beneficial interest into the sole name of her son who subsequently seeks to turn her out after a row. Is it enough simply to say to the son that he must abstain from interfering with the right of occupation of his mother, or is it necessary for the mother to enlist the help of trustees, lawyers and the courts in order to assert her positive rights? Under existing law, the only way in which the mother's beneficial rights in property to which she had unequally contributed could be safeguarded was if the court could find that a trust for sale existed on the facts of the case.[11] Yet, a trust for sale in these circumstances could only arise under the law if there was in existence either a trust instrument created by the mother or if the provisions of the Law of Property applied.[12] Neither situation existed in the case of *Bull* v. *Bull*. Yet Lord Denning famously glossed over these legal requirements to positively assert the mother's rights over her son.[13] He held that a trust for sale must exist in every case of an equitable tenancy in common and that this trust will be an implied or statutory trust of the legal estate on behalf of the parties in proportion to their contributions.[14] What this tells us is that property is a creature of the law. But it also tells us that law-makers may define property to embrace legal integrity by promoting social justice for all its citizens.

Judicial Discretion and Property Rights

If judicial discretion may be used to structure property rights, upon what theoretically coherent and practically valid basis may such discretion be exercised? Lawyers have to address this question if consistency in decision-making is to be achieved. To this end, a theory of property rights is helpful. This means that lawyers have a particular responsibility to understand the issues surrounding the institution of property because, uniquely, they have the responsibility to respond professionally, in a way that few professionals can, to the needs and anxieties of people who rely upon property, as one of the main goods of life, for a truly fulfilling existence in modern industrialized, and post-industrialized, democracies. Lawyers cannot therefore avoid or overlook issues of discretion and decision-making in this process. Whereas a case like *Bull* v. *Bull* tells us how judicial discretion can be exercised against all odds to protect the rights of someone who, strictly speaking, had no such rights at all under the law, it does not tell us what the theoretical basis is for the protection of equitable rights in property in such cases. Judges need to think about this; otherwise their decisions may not only lack coherence in the long run, but may fail to uphold the principle of legal integrity.

This is nowhere better exemplified than in the case of *Midland Bank Trust Company Ltd* v. *Green*.[15] Here the highest court in the land approached the issue of judicial discretion as if it had nothing whatsoever to do with justice and integrity in the law. The facts were that a father, having granted his son an option to purchase the land, then sought to deprive him of his interest some years later by conveying to his own wife that interest for a mere nominal sum, upon discovering that the son had not yet registered his option, even though the son had by then become a tenant in occupation of the land with his wife and family. In the House of Lords, Lord Wilberforce, who gave the only substantial speech, had no doubt that the son could be turned out. As a commercial equitable interest falling within one of the classes of registrable interest under the Land Charges Act 1925 the son's option had to be registered.[16] It was not for the courts to attempt to intervene even if in a particular case justice required such intervention by the courts. Lord Wilberforce overruled the Court of Appeal's finding in favour of the son and appeared to suggest that the judicial process could be blind to considerations of justice for the sake of certainty and clarity in the law:

> The case is plain: the Act is clear and definite. Intended as it was to provide a simple and understandable system for the protection of title to land, it should not be read down or glossed: to do so would destroy the usefulness of the Act. Any temptation to remould the Act to meet the facts of the present case, on the assumption that it *is a hard one and that justice requires it*, is, for me at least, removed by the consideration that the Act itself provides a simple and

> effective protection for persons in [the son's] position – viz. – by registration. (Emphases added.)[17]

Yet if there is an argument for integrity in the law, it does not make sense to say that there was no requirement for a party to a transaction to act in good faith, and indeed, many European systems of law do require parties to act in good faith when transacting. But the Court went further than it had to in favouring a sharp dealing by a party to that party's exclusive benefit, and to the other's palpable detriment. The Lords' solidly common-law based approach, which allows people to profiteer ruthlessly, was apparent in the following *dicta* of Lord Wilberforce:

> Addition of a requirement that the purchaser should be in good faith *would bring with it the necessity of inquiring into the purchaser's motives and state of mind.* The present case is a good example of the difficulties which would exist. If the position was simply that the purchaser had notice of the option, and decided nevertheless to buy the land, relying on the absence of notification, nobody could contend that she would be lacking in good faith. She would merely be taking advantage of a situation, which the law has provided, and the addition of a profit motive could not create an absence of good faith. *But suppose, and this is the respondent's argument, the purchaser's motive is to defeat the option, does this make any difference? Any advantage to oneself seems necessarily to involve a disadvantage for another*: to make the validity of the purchase depend upon which aspect of the transaction was prevalent in the purchaser's mind seems to create distinctions equally difficult to analyse in law as to establish in fact: *avarice and malice may be distinct sins, but in human conduct they are liable to be intertwined.* (Emphases added.)[18]

However, courts daily try to 'create distinctions equally difficult to analyse in law as to establish in fact'. Lord Wilberforce's judgment overlooks the role of judicial discretion in the reaching of fair decisions by courts of law[19] and ignores the fact that this is precisely what judges concerning themselves with social and moral justice do every day of the week. The Court gave property an immoral basis because Lord Wilberforce declared that the purchaser of property did not have to act in good faith. What did this mean in real terms? Here was a case where a father and a mother had acted in bad faith solely in order to divest a son of existing property rights in the land.[20] Surely, where justice was concerned this was a situation which the exercise of judicial discretion *alone* could address. His Lordship, however, thought that, provided that the purchaser had acted in accordance with the mechanics of contract and conveyance, then moral arguments had no role whatsoever in defining property rights because the purchaser 'would merely be taking advantage of a situation, which the law has provided, and the addition of a profit motive could not create an absence of good faith'.[21] However, this ignores the fact that discretion individualizes decision-making in every case. The courts cannot disable themselves from the task of exercising their discretion by a simple rule and rote application of the mechanical rules. They have to consider where strict law ends and discretion begins if they are to do justice in every case. In fact, this is precisely what happened in the Court of Appeal, where Lord Denning had gone so far as to say that the protection of the Land Charges Act of 1925 was *not available* in a case of fraud which covered 'any dishonest dealing done so as to deprive unwary innocents of their rightful dues'.[22] *Green* was a transfer of property rights in the context of a family arrangement where the exercise of judgment was concerned.

Even one hundred years ago the limitations of strict law were apparent to one such as Atkin LJ who, when considering family arrangements, observed that these arrangements could not be ignored because they

> are outside the realm of contracts altogether. The common law does not regulate the form of agreements between spouses. Their promises are not sealed with seals and sealing wax. The consideration that really obtains for them is that natural love and affection which counts for so little in these cold courts . . . *The parties themselves are advocate, judges, courts, sheriff's officer and reporter*. In respect of these promises *each house is a domain into which the King's writ does not seek to run*, and which its officers do not seek to be admitted.[23]

This makes clear the power of discretion. Even though a right may be wholly lacking in the clarity of definition ascribed by the law, it may still qualify as a right to property. All that decision-makers need do is to think more closely about the purposes to which the exercise of their discretion may be put. How can they meet the needs of modern society, and how much do they need to think about the parameters of the law that constrains them? Decision-makers need not be intellectually hide-bound. They can start by thinking about discretion separately from the judgment or decision itself. The question then is: To what purposes may the exercise of discretion be put and how may it best be exercised in the circumstances?

In recent years, this question has been nowhere more pressing than in the context of family property. Where property is conveyed to a spouse as a sole beneficial owner but the other makes contributions to the equity value by way of home improvements, should there be an agreement or a common intention between the parties before a resulting trust will be implied?[24] And if so, will this be ascertained at the time of the initial purchase? Further, can the courts ascribe to the parties intentions which they demonstrably never had? Depending on how a decision-maker uses and employs his discretion (as distinct from his decision) very different answers can be found to these questions. For example, in *Cowcher* v. *Cowcher*,[25] Bagnal J held that in order for a wife to acquire an interest in property, there had to be a consensus as to the proper shares in which the parties were to be taken as having provided the purchase money where there had been contributions to mortgage repayments. However, in *In re Densham*,[26] Goff J disagreed to hold that 'in the vast majority of cases, parties do not direct their minds to treating the money payments as notionally other than they are'. Goff J thought that the court should be able, in practical terms, to draw whichever inference it wanted and that it would be unconscionable for a party to set up the statute (s. 53(1)(b) of the LPA 1925) and repudiate an agreement as to 'interest consensus' that could be established in evidential terms.

Judges and decision-makers can only face up to their discretion if they rid themselves of the age-old philosophy that laws are only declared and not made by decision-makers. As anyone familiar with dispute resolution knows, this is the best kept myth of the judicial process. If it were remotely true advocates would not spend their early years perfecting their art of persuasion and would be soon out of work. Once this myth is debunked decision-makers can look to their discretion with a view to developing a theory of rights that fairly and accurately reflects the need for society to guarantee a sphere where the individual is inviolable and invulnerable. They may come to consider private property as one of the goods of final consumption which is vital to individuals having any individuality at all. In this way, the right to private property may be seen as a *public* right, where values other than private values, such as self-respect, dignity and integrity, have to be embraced by the judicial process.

But how should judges embrace these values? It is suggested that they should address questions of citizenship rights at the present time. They should concern themselves with serious social issues of the day that are at the heart of citizenship concerns and form the basis of integrity in our law. I have tried to pose this question in relation to my other work on immigrant rights. The question is the same: to what extent can groups that exist on the periphery of society be given a sense of belonging to the body politic? What is the role of law in giving every person a stake in society? To what extent may citizenship be remodelled as a concept of compelling contemporary relevance to this end? In this way, I have tried to suggest that law may be used as a medium of outreach, through a shared social status of citizenship, to vulnerable and underserved populations, in a way that eventually benefits the entire body politic. It is plain, from the experience of illiberal and authoritarian societies throughout the world, that a judicial process is all the poorer for its failure and inability to address these wider concerns of developing citizenship rights in the public interest.

Yet, in the United States the failure of Congress in the 1950s and 1960s to address citizenship and social justice issues such as racial segregation did not mean that the Supreme Court did not feel able to deal with such injustices.[27] Similarly, the record of the Indian Supreme Court in the 1970s and 1980s has also been very distinguished precisely because of its ability to address issues of social justice.[28] Of course, the British system of law and politics is different. But it is still concerned with issues of social justice in the same way. Further, it is not so different that it does not, like these other two great countries, subscribe to the doctrine of Separation of Powers that allows the courts to address these issues in their own right. Once it is accepted, as it must now be, that the courts in all three countries do not just slavishly and mechanically expound the law – and this has been markedly true of the British system throughout the 1980s and 1990s, with a series of leading appellate court decisions against the Government that can rival any under a written constitution – then it must be legitimate for the higher courts in Britain to address broader issues of social and public policy that help ensure legal integrity in the judicial process. Put another way, the higher courts cannot ignore and be wilfully blind to those questions when they decide individual cases on appeal to them. British judges need to think about property issues as citizenship concerns. What will this mean?

Using Citizenship to Structure Property Rights

Citizenship is today a central concept in democratic societies. The most important political problem that faces Britain at the end of the twentieth century is how the concept of citizenship can be given a contemporary meaning in a liberal democratic society. To say that citizenship can be defined as participation in or membership of a community does not answer the question. How fully can or do individuals participate? What does membership of a community precisely mean? If decision-makers adjudicating over property disputes have a sense of appreciation about these issues, can or should they contribute through the legal process to the attainment by individuals of full citizenship rights as equals? Most people would not consider property rights to be central today to the idea of citizenship in the state. In the modern democratic state, people participate as citizens by exercising their political power through the electoral process. Once they participate in this manner they are assured of their legal membership of a political community in which they live and which is based upon the ideal of universal suffrage and their membership of the civil community that is underpinned by the rule of law.

This popular idea of modern citizenship implies that people are equal before the law across the social structure. What this idea overlooks, however, is the social inequality of classes in a market economy. This inequality has a direct bearing on their practical ability to exercise citizenship rights as individual members of a civil community. Citizenship *per se* therefore does not guarantee rights. The masterly analysis of T. H. Marshall in his *Citizenship and Social Class*[29] focuses precisely on the relationship of citizenship with the class system. Marshall advocated a universal and egalitarian-based notion of citizenship. He focused on the nature of citizenship in post-Second World War Britain and his analysis is particularly compelling because it follows the rise of the welfare state. He helpfully traces the emergence of citizenship in the modern nation state through the historical development of capitalist society. He is astute to recognize the contradiction between the equality of status in citizenship at one level of society and the inequality of class capitalism at the other end of society. For judges, this means that they can treat property rights as being integral to the maintenance of current market and class relations or they can exercise their discretion to further the ends of citizenship by deciding that a widely dispersed private ownership of property is the surest foundation for a stable and liberal democracy. They can thus treat property as a springboard for citizenship and political liberty in the state.

For judges, Marshall's understanding of citizenship can provide clear guidance. He saw full citizenship not only as a status which is attached to full membership of the community but also as a status where those associated with it have equal rights and duties. Marshall distanced himself from the conventional idea that membership of a community is basically a political matter. He considered that citizenship comprises civil, political and social rights. Citizenship should be understood in terms of rights and in terms of the institutional context through which the rights are exercised. To that extent, an understanding of citizenship and its correlative rights can inform an understanding of the expectations of people as citizens.

Marshall maintained that the civil aspect of citizenship is that aspect which is essentially to do with the rights that are necessary for the enjoyment of individual citizens, and that the decisions of the courts and law are the institutions that serve to protect these rights. The political aspect of citizenship is that aspect which is to do with the right to participate in the exercising of political power, and the social aspect is that aspect which is to do with the standard of life currently obtainable and to the social heritage of society. He developed this argument by showing that capitalism has evolved as a social system with the class structure developing within it. Citizenship for him was no longer a system of rights which arose out of market relations, but now in the modern state a system of rights that stands opposed to market and class systems.[30]

This contribution of Marshall surely demonstrates how different a discretion based on a theory of citizenship rights is going to be for judges than one based on traditional common-law grounds. Marshall began from the idea that citizenship is a status implying full membership of a community and that those having this status are equal in terms of their rights and duties. This was the conventional idea of citizenship, and Marshall argued that different societies will attach different rights and duties to the status of citizenship as there is no universal principle of rights and duties. However, Marshall then went further than this and said that if one goes beyond this conventional idea and notes that membership of a community is primarily a *political* matter, one can see that there are three aspects to rights of citizenship: the social, political and civil rights.

Marshall's contribution lies in the observance that the different aspects of citizenship have different institutional bases with quite different histories. The different aspects of citizenship may have very different relation to each other because of their quite different composite parts impacting differently on distinct social groups. It is because of this observation that it is argued in this work that the courts, when upholding citizenship rights, must expressly set out to promote social rights in Britain, in the way that the American and Indian Supreme Courts have done as a result of their respective legislatures' failure to address these issues through the democratic process. Legislatures can indeed sometimes make the mistake of assuming that citizenship rights are deducible from civil rights. Marshall's position is clear that, contrary to the customary view, not all citizenship rights are actually derivable from civil rights, particularly from property rights as conventionally understood. Under conventional liberal theory it is true that social as well as political rights are deducible from the institution of market-based private property. Ever since John Locke, liberal theory has stated that these rights are extendable to non-property classes once their labour assumes the status of property which they own. But Marshall argues that rights are not always a secondary product of other rights and that in this case rights can attach quite independently of others to the status of citizenship. Citizenship rights, in their various composite forms, are necessarily therefore in a state of flux, like all societal norms, and courts of law must respond to the current social, political and civil rights that are integral to citizenship.

Once courts of law decide to respond in this way, they can help to integrate a society into a stable community of equals. Socially disruptive inequalities between different classes based on material condition can be dispersed if there is an equal participation by all in the life of the community and citizenship has an integrative function that can equalize status for its members. Property has always been critical to full citizenship rights. People who are today having their houses repossessed by mortgage companies are not going to feel full citizens of the community in which they live. Mortgage repossessions often end in the courts. The courts should not wait for a lead on this point from the legislature because, historically, the record of the legislature in Britain is not impressive in conferring equal property rights as a way of promoting citizenship rights. The British Parliament has not historically rushed to promulgate legislation to help integrate society on an equal footing. In fact, the evidence shows that property was used as an institution to help maintain citizenship inequalities. This is why the courts must act.

Thus, the First Reform Act of 1832 was hardly very significant in modern democratic terms because it left five out of six adult males without the vote. The Second Reform Act of 1867 was the enactment that is today generally accredited with bringing about the political incorporation of the English working class and it is a good example of how suffrage can be used in the integrative process.[31] The effect of this enactment was to more than double the electorate from one to two and a half million voters by giving the vote to all householders in the parliamentary boroughs, thereby including urban working-class men in the suffrage. However, the central importance of property in this integrative process was unmistakable and is still often overlooked. As E. P. Thompson states in *England in the Nineteenth Century*, 'The prevailing eighteenth century theory still held the ground – that it is property and not people which ought to be represented in Parliament. Only the growing movement of Radicals held that men should have votes as men and as citizens, and not as the owners of specified quantities of landed property.'[32] The 1867 Act changed the political rights of those in the urban boroughs, but it left agricultural workers and industrial workers, such as miners, in the rural counties completely unaffected. This deficiency was addressed by the Reform Acts of 1884–85, which developed the integrative process, by making the county franchise the same as that of the towns, thus giving the vote to farm labourers and previously excluded miners. The electorate was increased from about three to five million. Yet, it is only with the Representation of the People Act 1915 that the adult population, which did not include women under 30, was given the vote. This was a major advance given that, prior to the 1918 Act, only half of the male urban working class had the vote. However, even though political rights were extended during the nineteenth century and the 1918 Act attached these rights to citizenship rather than to property, the different status of men and women under 30 and anomaly rural voting had yet to be eliminated until the universal franchise of 1928 and the equal franchise of 1948.

What this historical excursus shows is that the levelling of rights to the legislative process is not enough if people are unable, because of their inherently unequal position in society, to avail themselves of such rights. If the emphasis was simply on formal equality under the law then those that exist on the periphery of society would not easily be able to come into the mainstream without the supportive role of the institutional structures of society. What the period of electoral and political reform of the nineteenth century does show is that it was conducted by the British Establishment with full anticipation of its likely outcome. The British Establishment sponsored the extension of the suffrage piecemeal in such a way that the newly integrated sections of the population felt unable to threaten the political system which they had just been allowed to enter. In this way, the British Establishment consolidated its own political position. Soon the system of public elementary education was established, the civil service and the army were reorganized and the law was overhauled as well.[33] The initiative for reform lay always with the ruling class, which acted out of self-interest. As Ralph Miliband records, 'in the context of a solid parliamentary and political system decisively shaped by the forces of property, the extension of the suffrage was more an act of containment than emancipation'.[34] This was because the new urban proletariat was regarded as a threat by the ruling class. They thought that its piecemeal and selective political incorporation would reduce the possibility of violent revolution of the kind that had been witnessed on the continent of Europe.

The ruling class changed the essential institutional forms but not the differential distribution of power in society. The secret ballot, introduced in England in 1872, neutralized the threat of emergent working-class organizations by isolating the individual working-class voter both from his superiors and, more importantly, from his peers. The result was, as Simon Clarke explains, that

> The extension of the franchise was not intended to admit the working class to the Constitution, but to bring into the electoral game those who exhibited moral reliability and political responsibility, qualities measured by respect for property and the Constitution and found among the more affluent, and correspondingly improved, sections of the working class, but which were defined by moral and not economic terms.[35]

This analysis shows that if judges are to engage in the integrative process today they will have to do it in a way that is less cynical than their parliamentary forebears. They will have to base the integrative process less on a respect for property and more on a respect for citizenship rights. They must move towards an idea of moral property. This they can do only if they are prepared to view property as a basis for the redistribution of wealth in pursuit of a larger realization of citizenship rights in the community as a whole. Citizenship has a role in the integration of society because it has a special significance for participation in social life. Citizenship is not merely an equalization of rights in the formal sense but involves something much more substantial. It is a real membership of a real community.

To that extent, judges will have to develop an equalitarian approach which may be defined as an approach which has less to do with power in the state (and its consolidation) and more to do with seeking and achieving stability in society through treating every individual as being of an equal moral worth by virtue of his or her human integrity. It is accepted that this is not the conventional role of the law from a historical perspective. As Professor E. P. Thompson states:

> [T]he law is, perhaps more clearly than any other cultural or institutional artifact, by definition a part of a 'superstructure' adopting itself to the necessities of an infrastructure of productive forces and productive relations. As such, it is clearly an instrument of the *de facto* ruling class: it both defines and defends these rulers' claims upon resources and labour power – it says what shall be property and what shall be crime – and it mediates class relations with a set of appropriate rules and sanctions, all of which, ultimately, confirm and consolidate existing class power. Hence the rule

> of law is only another mask for a rule of class. The revolutionary can have no interest in law, unless as a phenomenon of the ruling class power and hypocrisy; it should be his aim simply to overthrow it.[36]

This work does not reject the law but rather calls for its utilization in a form that is an effective instrument for social justice. Provided that there is a framework for moral property in place, the legal delineation of property rights by the courts is surely to be welcomed if it is based on egalitarian ideals. In the next chapter, we consider how some of the major problems of property law adjudication have been determined recently by the courts in this country.

Notes and References

1 Friedman, Milton (1962) *Capitalism and Freedom*, p. 10. Chicago.
2 Nozick, Robert (1974) *Anarchy, State and Utopia*, pp. 158ff. Oxford.
3 A similar view has been put forward by John Rawls. See Rawls, John (1971) *A Theory of Justice*. Oxford.
4 Tawney, R. A. (1924) *The Acquisitive Society*. London.
5 See *A Theory of Justice*, *supra*, pp. 258–74.
6 See Arendt, Hannah (1961) *Between Past and Future*. London; and Wolin, Sheldon (1961) *Politics and Vision*. Boston.
7 405 U.S. 538, 552 (1972). At this point Justice Stewart referred expressly to Locke and Blackstone.
8 As John Locke said, 'for I truly have no property in that which another can by right take from me, when he pleases, against my consent'. See Locke, John (1967) *Two Treatises of Civil Government*, pp. 378–9. Cambridge.
9 Honore, A. M. (1977) Ownership. *Oxford Essays in Jurisprudence*, p. 113. Oxford.
10 [1955] 1 QB 234. The house was intended to be a home for both the parties. When the son later married it was agreed that the mother would occupy two rooms in the house and that the son and his wife would occupy the remainder.
11 Under s. 34(1) 'an undivided share in land shall not be capable of being created except as provided by the Settled Land Act 1925 or as hereinafter mentioned'. However, the statutory provisions here did not create a trust for sale.
12 Thus, s. 36(1) (to which s. 34 applied) did not provide for a trust for sale in a situation where the equitable interest in land was held by tenants in common. S. 36(1) reads that 'where a legal estate (not being settled land) is beneficially limited to or held in trust *for any persons as joint tenants*, the same shall be held on trust for sale ... ' (emphasis added). In this case both mother and son had contributed to the purchase price in unequal sums. However, Denning LJ gave a strained construction to s. 36(4) of the Settled Land Act 1925 and applied it to this situation so that a trust for sale would exist in every case of equitable tenancy in common. S. 36(4) states that '[a]n undivided share in land shall not be capable of being created except under a trust instrument or under the Law of Property Act 1925, and shall then only take effect behind a trust for sale'.
13 As Lord Denning explained, 'the rights of equitable tenants in common as between

themselves have never, so far as I know, been defined; but there is plenty of authority about the rights of legal owners in common. Each of them is entitled to the possession of the land and to the use and enjoyment of it in a proper manner. Neither can turn out the other; but if one of them should take more than his proper share the injured party can bring an action for an account. If one of them should go so far as to oust the other he is guilty of a trespass . . . Such being the rights of legal tenants in common, I think that the rights of equitable owners in common are the same, save only for such differences as are necessarily consequent on the interest being equitable and not legal' (p. 237).

14 In *Barclay* v. *Barclay* [1970] 2 QB 677, fifteen years after Lord Denning gave his judgment in *Bull* v. *Bull*, his Lordship explained that decision by stating that 'in *Bull* v. *Bull* the prime object of the trust was that the parties should occupy the house together. They were entitled to the possession of it in undivided shares. That made them, in equity, tenants in common. An equitable tenancy in common arises whenever two or more persons become entitled to the possession of property (or the rents and profits thereof) in undivided shares. They may become so entitled by agreement, or under a will, or by reference, as often happens when husband and wife acquire their matrimonial home. The legal owner holds the legal estate on trust for them as tenants in common' (p. 684).

15 [1981] AC 513.

16 The Option was, in legal terms, an estate contract and so a legal charge, Class C, within the meaning of the Land Charges Act 1925, and the correct and statutory method for protecting such an option was to enter it in the Register of the Land Charges, maintained under the Land Charges Act 1925. Under s. 13(2) of the said Act: 'a land charge of Class B, Class C or Class D, created or arising after the commencement of this Act, shall . . . *be void as against a purchaser of the land charged therewith* . . . unless the land charge is registered in the appropriate Register before the completion of the purchase . . . .' (Emphasis added.)

17 *Supra*, note 15, p. 529.

18 *Ibid.*, p. 531. For a discussion of the requirement of good faith in property transaction, see Juss, Satvinder, Human rights and the adversarial individual interest in contracts: a case study of good faith in property transactions. *Essays in European Law and Israel* (ed. A. M. Rabello), pp. 769–80. Jerusalem.

19 For a commentary on this case, see (1980) 96 LQR, p. 8; (1981) CLJ, p. 213; (1981) CONV, p. 361; (1981) 97 LQR, p. 518; and (1985) CLJ, p. 280.

20 The case is also a good example of the effects of non-registration, which had previously been commented upon by Professor Wade: see (1956) CLJ 216, pp. 226–28.

21 *Supra*, note 18.

22 [1980] Ch. 590, p. 625.

23 See *Balfour* v. *Balfour* [1919] 2 KB 571, p. 579.

24 As Browne-Wilkinson VC asked in *Grant* v. *Edwards* [1986] Ch. 638, without however answering the question: 'does there have to be positive evidence that the claimants did the acts in conscious reliance on the common intention? Does the court have to be satisfied that she would not have done the acts relied on, but for the common intention, e.g. would not the claimant have contributed to the household expenses out of affection for the legal owner and as part of their joint life together even if she had no interest in the house? Do the acts relied on as detriment have to

be inherently referable to the house, e.g. contribution to the purchase or physical labour on the house?' (p. 656).

25 [1972] 1 WLR 425. See also a discussion of this case by Levin, Jennifer (1972) *Modern Law Review* (35), 547.

26 [1975] 1 WLR 1519, p. 1525.

27 See Bickel, Alexander (1970) *The Supreme Court and the Idea of Progress*. New York. Also see Bickel, Alexander (1962) *The Least Dangerous Branch: The Supreme Court at the Bar of Politics*. Indianapolis. See now also Savage, David (1992) *Turning Right: The Making of the Rehnquist Supreme Court*. New York.

28 Thus, Baxi has recently described how directive principles have been used in India in the context of what is sometimes called 'public interest litigation', or what he prefers to term 'social action litigation': see Baxi, Upendra (1993) Judicial discourse: the dialectics of the face and the mask. *Journal of the Indian Law Institute* (35), 7.

29 Marshall, T. H. (1950) *Citizenship and Social Class and Other Essays*. Cambridge.

30 *Ibid.*, pp. 71–4, 84.

31 Although, as Moorhouse has argued, 'after Acts of 1867–8 at best *only* 30% of the male, adult, urban working class were enfranchised'. See Moorhouse, H. F. (1973) The political incorporation of the British working class: an interpretation. *Sociology* (7), 3.

32 Thompson, E. P. (1975) *England in the Nineteenth Century*, p. 22. London.

33 Cole, G. D. H. and Postgate, R. (1946) *The Common People 1746–1946*, pp. 365–6. London.

34 Miliband, Ralph (1984) *Capitalist Democracy in Britain*, p. 25. Oxford.

35 Clarke, Simon (1982) *Marx, Marginalism and Modern Sociology*, p. 133. London.

36 Thompson, E. P. (1990) *Whigs and Hunters*, p. 259. London.

2

Mortgages and Co-owners

Property and law are born and must die together. Before the laws, there was no property: take away the laws, all property ceases.
Jeremy Bentham

Justice Frankfurter of the US Supreme Court believed that he could identify 'those liberties of the individual which history has attested as the indispensable conditions of an open as against a closed society' by a 'disinterested enquiry pursued in the spirit of science, on a balanced order of facts exactly and fairly stated, on the detached consideration of conflicting claims . . . on a judgment not *ad hoc* and episodic but duly mindful of reconciling the needs both of continuity and of change in a progressive society'.[1] In recent years, nothing has more vividly illustrated the tension in the conflicting claims for property rights in today's modern period of continuity and change than the problems caused by the now familiar consequence of bank or building society mortgage charges taken over a family home, by one co-owner partner at the instance of the other, in circumstances which are not evident to outsiders. This has raised a problem for the courts more of moral and socio-economic dimensions than of pure technical Land Law.

Historically, traditional English Land Law has not dealt elegantly with these problems. It has not, as Justice Frankfurter sought to do, identified individual liberties as a basis for an open society, through an inquiry on a balanced order of facts exactly and fairly stated. As Pollock and Maitland have noted only too well, the medieval notion of land tenure 'has dealt rudely with the facts, it has neglected many a distinction of great social and economic importance, it has driven its trenchant dilemmas through the middle of natural classes and athwart some lines of customary morality; but it has been bold and strong and therefore simple'.[2] Yet, this notion of boldness and strongness which favours oppressive bargaining and the exploitation of superior economic strength is misconceived for a legal system based on liberal democratic values. Economic rights are not necessarily or inherently paramount over other rights.

In the last chapter we saw that there is an analytic weakness in the distinction between economic and non-economic rights because it is not property that has rights but people who have rights, and one cannot overlook the importance of property and contract on protecting the dispossessed as well as the possessed. In assessing the property rights of mortgagees and co-owners the English courts have played a distinctive and at times distinguished role. In this, they have been ahead of Parliament. Judicial contributions to the development of legal rights, as has not been unusual in recent years, have far exceeded legislative contributions in the progressive development of legal rights. The policy shift in favour of manipulated partners was entirely judicial and was taken nearly twenty years ago in the seminal case of *Williams and Glyn's Bank* v. *Boland*[3] in 1981, and it was given a further impetus in the 1994 case of *Barclays Bank* v. *O'Brien*.[4] This chapter considers the discretion exercised by the courts in these and other related cases. It enquires whether the courts have exercised their discretion in an orderly and principled manner and whether they have managed to advance citizenship rights through the attainment of greater social justice.

The Discretion to Disregard Traditional Concepts of Property Law

Williams and Glyn's Bank Ltd v. *Boland*[5] is arguably the most important case in modern English Land Law. The case arose when the country was on the threshold of a long property boom. Yet this masked the difficulties of the 1970s. That decade had already seen high inflation and volatile interest rates. House prices had risen dramatically in relation to retail and share prices. Real property therefore came to be seen as the safest long-term investment. The rise in house prices meant that more home-owners and property purchasers began to take advantage of the escalating value of properties so that a second mortgage market grew with borrowers dealing with less well-known financial institutions. The result was an increased risk to borrowers, not least from the unconscionable imposition of harsh and oppressive mortgage terms. In addition, this property boom of the early 1970s was followed by a period of deep economic recession. There was an increase in unemployment, redundancy and bankruptcy and cases of mortgage default naturally began to rise. The time was ripe for the courts to police property transactions and to protect property rights.

The *Boland* case, therefore, arose in circumstances that were not entirely dissimilar to those pertaining in the early 1990s. *Boland* is important in having defined and articulated the rights of equitable owners in the property. It is important in having rejected the traditional doctrine of conversion in relation to the matrimonial home as being unreal. It is important in having analysed the rights of parties behind a trust for sale. And finally, it is important in its statement that lending institutions have a positive duty of enquiry in order to protect the rights of third parties whose claims may not be immediately apparent to the principal transacting parties. It is submitted that what *Boland* demonstrated most clearly is that there is in modern land law an egalitarian social contract which holds banks, society and owner-occupiers of property having legitimate rights and interests in a property-based economy, and it affirms the view that the aim of the law is to achieve a fair resolution of those interests in the face of highly unequal relationships between these interests. In this way individual members of society have been made to feel full citizens of a society where institutional bodies wield much economic power.

The issues in *Boland* arose when two sides brought consolidated appeals to the Court of Appeal. They argued that they had both been living in their respective matrimonial homes when their husbands, each of whom was acting as a single statutory trustee for sale, had charged their matrimonial home to the plaintiff bank so as to be able to raise loans for various business enterprises. The bank had made no enquiry as to the possibility that either of the wives may have a beneficial interest in the property so charged. Although both wives had a beneficial interest behind an implied trust for sale neither had protected their interest by entering it on the Land Register as a 'minor interest'.[6] The bank claimed possession of the charged property when the husbands' respective businesses went into liquidation and each wife concerned then claimed adverse interests in their respective matrimonial home. Since the wives had failed to register their interest it was clear that they would lose out to the bank who had the charge unless the courts could hold that their beneficial interests under the statutory trusts were 'overriding interests'.[7]

At first instance, Templeman J had held that a beneficiary, such as a wife, behind a trust for sale, having failed to protect her interest on the Land Register as a minor interest, could not fall back on the protection afforded by the general category of 'overriding interests' in the Land Registration Act 1925. Such a view clearly had considerable legal force because under a system of registered land legal efficacy was only given to those interests that were entered on the Register, and the exceptions of 'overriding interests' were only created because they comprised interests that were either of particular social importance or created particular conveyancing difficulties, so as to exempt them from the requirements of registration. Templeman J pointed out that where the interests could be registered they should be registered. A failure to do so would damage the scheme of the Act. Well-known previous cases, such as *Bridges* v. *Mees*[8] and *Hodgson* v. *Marks*,[9] where a beneficiary behind a trust had been able to claim an overriding interest, were all cases concerning a 'bare trust' and not a trust for sale, and in those cases it had not been open to the beneficiary to register their interest as a minor interest on the Land Register.

For Templeman J it did not make sense to categorize an interest as an 'overriding interest' when it could and should, properly speaking, have been protected by entry on the Register either as a beneficial interest or as a statutory 'right of occupation' under the Matrimonial Homes Act 1967. To allow this to happen 'would really make that Act a nonsense provided that the legal owner could say or allege at any time that he or she had contributed to the purchase price. The position which would result from that . . . would be quite intolerable.' Templeman J thought that the legal provisions in that case would be used as a device for a fraudulent purpose. It would only require one co-owner partner to collude with the other and falsely say that they had jointly contributed to the matrimonial home. They could succeed in defrauding their creditors simply by putting up an elaborate design of a fictitious claim for beneficial entitlements, by one spouse who had not in actual fact contributed and not seen fit to register their interest as a minor interest on the Register.[10]

In the Court of Appeal and the House of Lords, however, these concerns of Templeman J were swept aside. Here judicial discretion was exercised rather differently. In purely legal terms, it may be argued that Templeman J's position was eminently and impeccably well put and beyond reproach. However, the Appeal Courts did not take a purely legal view of the situation before them. Indeed, there is clear evidence that they saw it first and foremost as a social situation requiring the solution of a social problem that had long gone unredressed. This called for a radical and activist exercise of judicial discretion. The Court of Appeal, presided over by Lord Denning, had no difficulty in concluding that the Matrimonial Homes Act 1967 had 'no relevance'[11] to the matter under consideration, and in the House of Lords, Lord Wilberforce was emphatic that the appeals do 'not involve any question of matrimonial law, or to the rights of married women or women as such'.[12] Both Appeal Courts declared that beneficial interests behind statutory trusts for sale could be described as 'overriding interests' under Section 70(i)(g) of the Land Registration Act 1925. However, even under that law this protection only crystallizes in respect of 'the rights of every person in actual occupation' and it was in respect of this question that the Appeal Courts made their most important contribution.

In examining this question the Courts clearly had to mediate between the social interests of the family and the economic interests of the lending institution, particularly as the latter may have made an enquiry of the former but been unable to discover latent beneficial interests behind a statutory trust for sale. This may apply clearly to a wife or to other members of the extended family who are part of the family unit that had contributed to the family home but did not have their names on the legal title. Should the bank or building society, in the uncompromising commercial world, be under an obligation to make enquiries of these other members? Or should it not be enough in legal terms to make an enquiry of the person in whose name the property is vested? Both Appeal Courts took a socially sensitive approach. The speeches in both Courts display considerable moral force and conviction. The Court of Appeal was unanimous in its view that a wife's occupation is not a shadow of occupation of the owner of the property. Lord Denning was dismissive of this as describing the law 'a hundred years ago when the law regarded husband and wife as one: and the husband as that one'.[13] He had no doubt that

> most wives are now joint owners of the matrimonial home – in law or in equity – with their husbands . . . Visit the home and you will find that she is in personal occupation of it just as much as he is. She eats there and sleeps there just as he does. She is in control of all that goes on there – just as much as he. In no respect whatsoever does the nature of her occupation differ from his . . . [14]

In the Court of Appeal, Lord Denning had little sympathy with the idea that a judicial concern with social justice would imperil commercial life. He did not feel that the Courts' decision

> [s]hould cause any difficulty to conveyancers. Nor should it impair the proper conduct of businesses. Anyone who lends money on the security of a matrimonial home nowadays ought to realise that the wife may have a share in it. He ought to make sure that the wife agrees to it, or to go to the house and make enquiries of her. It seems to me utterly wrong, that the lender should turn a blind eye to the wife's interests or the possibility of it – and afterwards seek to turn her and the family out on the plea that he did not know that she was in actual occupation.[15]

Indeed, in a different context, *Birkom Investments Limited* v. *Carr*

Limited, Lord Denning, when faced with the argument that the Courts' decision would 'cause chaos and confusion amongst conveyancers, no-one buying property would know where he stood', had replied: 'I am not disturbed by those forebodings. I prefer to see that justice is done; and let the conveyancers look after themselves.'[16] In *Boland* Lord Denning was harsh in his criticism of the bank in having overlooked the moral and social dimension to its role in society. He declared:

> If a bank is to do its duty, in the society in which we live, *it should recognise the integrity of the matrimonial home.* It should not destroy it by disregarding the wife's interest in it – simply to ensure that it is the husband's debt in full – with the high interest rate now prevailing . . . *We should not give monied might priority over social justice* . . . Each of the wives is entitled to be protected in her occupation of the matrimonial home. The bank is not entitled to throw these families out into the street – simply to get the last penny of the husband's debt.[17] (Emphases added.)

Ormrod LJ similarly discarded the conveyancing difficulties heavily stressed by the bank. The banks could not ignore the social realities of life that faced them:

> [C]o-ownership is becoming increasingly popular. Building societies and other institutions that finance house purchase are familiar with it and, if necessary, can protect themselves by requiring the spouse of the purchaser to join in the purchase and mortgage. The people who, on the whole, seem more likely to be affected, are those who advance money on the security of the domestic property either in the form of overdrafts or other loans, and those legal proprietors who wish to raise money on their homes. In these days, the word 'chaos' is a strong word to describe the plight of such persons who have only got to get the consent of the co-owners, or forgo a transaction gravely prejudicial to the co-owner. So, with some trepidation, I venture to doubt whether the success of the wives will really have such catastrophic consequences. If, on the other hand, they fail the result will certainly be catastrophic for them and many like them.[18]

The beauty of the Court of Appeal's judgment in *Boland* is that it expressly rejects the notion that the disparities in the social and economic distribution of power in society can only be adjusted to the operation of normal market forces. Rather, the courts have a pivotal role to play in fashioning social policy and in using the law to effect important social change. In *Boland* the courts assumed centre stage and adopted a markedly enlightened approach to social policy.

In the House of Lords, Lord Wilberforce further left no doubt that questions of social justice are inherent in the judicial process and are the central basis of the judicial function. His Lordship recognized that requiring conveyancers to make enquiries of third parties might 'add to the burdens of purchasers, and involve them in enquiries which in some cases may be troublesome'. However, he saw nothing wrong with this:

> What is involved is a departure from an easygoing practice of dispensing with enquiries as to occupation beyond that of the vendor and accepting the risks of doing so. To substitute for this a practice of more careful enquiry as to the fact of occupation, and if necessary, as to the rights of occupiers, cannot ... be considered as unacceptable except at the price of overlooking the widespread development of shared interests of co-ownership ... *I cannot believe that Parliament intended this*.[19] (Emphasis added.)

Lord Scarman, for his part, perhaps put it best when he implicitly adverted to the shared common enterprise of society at large based on modestly egalitarian social contract between all concerned:

> Nor must the courts flinch when assailed by arguments to the effect that the protection of (a third party) interest may create difficulties in banking or conveyancing practice. The difficulties are, I believe, exaggerated *but bankers and solicitors exist to provide the service that the public needs*. They can – as they have successfully done in the past – adjust their practice, if it be socially required ... [I]t is our duty ... to give the provisions, if we properly can, a meaning which will work for, rather than against, the rights conferred by Parliament, or recognised by judicial decision, as being necessary for the achievement of social justice.[20] (Emphasis added.)

In this statement, Lord Scarman reflected a truism which is often forgotten. If the legal result of the decision, through the rule and rote application of the law, is manifestly unjust then it cannot be morally and socially irrelevant to the proper exercise of judicial discretion. Thus the courts move to an idea of moral property. As Lord Scarman said:

> The courts *may not ... put aside as irrelevant* the undoubted fact that, if the two wives succeed, the protection of the

> beneficial interest which English law now recognises that a married woman has in the matrimonial home will be strengthened whereas if they lose this interest can be weakened and even destroyed by an unscrupulous husband.[21] (Emphasis added.)

However, in seeking to attain social justice the House of Lords perhaps went too far, because it is arguable that in its concern for vulnerable third parties in the matrimonial home the court overlooked justice for the bank. Notwithstanding the commendable policy objectives that both the Court of Appeal and the House of Lords diligently sought to attain in the judicial process, it cannot be forgotten that this was a case where both wives had had the clear option of registering their beneficial interest on the Register but had failed to do so thereby causing an unnecessary detriment to the lending financial institution. It cannot be overlooked that neither was involved in a matrimonial dispute with their respective spouses. It cannot be overlooked that their spouses were clearly able to deny the legitimate rights of their creditors by a dubious reliance on the equitable rights of their wives' interests that remained unregistered. And finally, it cannot be overlooked that all of this was done on the basis of the argument – not that the wives were unaware that their husbands had charged the matrimonial home over to the bank – but that the bank had failed to make any enquiry of them.

Subject to these criticisms, which are not insignificant, there is no getting away from the fact, however, that the judicial approach of the appellate courts in *Boland* stands as a shining example of radical judicial activism to protect vulnerable individual interests. This activism paved the way towards wider citizenship rights in the social community. The effect of this was to alter the strict requirements of Land Law that property lawyers are familiar with. Both courts discarded the strict requirements of legal principle in favour of social principle. Under the orthodox doctrine of conversion, a beneficiary under a trust for sale of land is deemed to have an interest in personalty and not in realty, even where that land has yet to be sold. This is clearly a fictional and fictitious idea. It did not conform to the reality of what the courts were facing in real life. Yet, the two wives in *Boland* would only have had an interest in the proceeds of the sale which their husbands' properties represented.

This was not a small matter of legal principle. The doctrine of conversion is intrinsic to the trust for sale where the trustees are always under an express duty to sell the land. To this extent, the interests of beneficiaries are necessarily monetized and never in the land. Even before the property is sold, Equity will look upon that as done which ought to be done and regard the beneficial interests as being in the monetary value only. From the beginning, Equity anticipates the eventual sale arising from the trustees' duty to sell with the result that the interest in the land is transformed into an interest in the money as soon as the trust is set up.[22] The historical reason for this doctrine of conversion is to give clarity and certainty to the devolution of interests that exist behind a trust for sale, and it is noteworthy that this in itself was a product of judicial discretion at a time when clarity and certainty in a more patriarchal and rigid society were more important legal policy objectives than the attainment of social justice. As a result, the question of the precise timing of the sale by the trustees was deliberately avoided in the exercise of judicial discretion. It was this doctrine of conversion that was questioned by the appellate courts in *Boland*. Lord Denning was at the front in his enquiry:

> What is the nature of this trust? It was suggested to us that it was not a trust of the house itself, but only a trust in the proceeds of the sale. That cannot be right. When a married man and his wife buy a house, they do it so as to live in it – so that it should be a home both for them and for their children – for the foreseeable future. They do not intend to sell it – not at any rate for many years hence ... *The couple do not have in mind a sale – nor a division of the proceeds of sale – except in the far distance.*[23] (Emphasis added.)

Ormrod LJ approached this question in the same way:

> In the instant cases, the object of the trust was to provide a joint home and the last thing the parties contemplated was that the house would be sold and the cash divided between them. In converting such a relationship into a trust for sale the legislation of 1925 created, in effect, a legal fiction ... This may have been an inescapable consequence of the method adopted to achieve its primary objective, that is, the simplification of conveyancing. But to press this legal fiction to its logical conclusion and beyond the point which is necessary to achieve the primary objective is not justifiable, particularly *when it involves the sacrifice of a class or classes of persons*.[24] (Emphasis added.)

Lord Wilberforce, in the House of Lords, did not have full arguments on the doctrine of conversion addressed to him. Nevertheless, he was of the opinion that 'to describe the interests of spouses in a house jointly bought to be lived in as a matrimonial home as merely an interest in proceeds of sale, or rents or profits until sale, *is just a little unreal*'[25] (emphasis added). Lord Scarman restricted the proper application of the doctrine of conversion by implying that it should only come into effect if and when the sale actually took place:

> It is conceded that each wife has a beneficial interest in the land which is her matrimonial home. Each is an equitable tenant in common behind a trust for sale, there being only one trustee, her husband, in whom the legal estate (a freehold) is vested. Each, therefore, enjoys by reason of her interest, a present right of occupation as well as a right to share in the proceeds of the sale if and when the house is sold: *Bull* v. *Bull* [1955] 1. Q.B. 234.[26]

In *Boland*, the higher courts rejected the application of the overworked doctrine of conversion to residential property holders on the grounds that it was ill-fitted to the realities of modern life and the courts did not consider themselves to be usurping the legislative function by pursuing particular policy objectives that had the overall effect of securing greater social justice in the community. Thus did the courts meet the demands of moral and social claims made upon them by vulnerable and underserved populations in the community. The courts declared that commercial and financial institutions had a positive duty to pursue their economic and profit-making ends in a morally and socially sensitive manner that does not damage the property rights of the weaker sections of society.

The Increasing Importance of Equity in the Modern Law

The 1925 legislation had two purposes: firstly, to overcome and prevent the fragmentation of title to land; and secondly, to reform property conveyancing by simplifying the mechanics of land transfer. The main statutes of the 1925 legislation are: the Settled Land Act 1925; the Law of Property Act 1925; the Land Charges Act 1925; and the Land Registration Act 1925. The modification of some aspects of traditional conveyancing practice of transfer by title deed was undertaken by the first three of these four Acts. The Land Registration Act brought about registered conveyancing by introducing a new system of conveyancing which was intended to speed up and simplify the process of land transfer since purchasers could more easily investigate the title that they were buying and discover the full extent, if any, of subsidiary rights that burdened the land. There has been little research undertaken on the history of the provisions in the 1925 legislation, but it is clear that these reforms are not setting out to address social needs and changes in society, which in any event did not come about until well into the twentieth century. They were not setting out to establish parity and equity in society.

Important recent research undertaken by Avner Offer appeared in his article 'The origin of the Law of Property Acts 1910–1925' in 1977[27] confirming this view, followed by his book *Property and Politics 1870–1914* which was published in 1981.[28] Offer suggested that the 1925 legislation was the product of a long-running battle between lawyers and the state for the control of land transfer. According to Offer, the legal profession had a vested interest in retaining the inefficient mechanisms which a rational reform of the law would do away with in the general social interest. A more recent work has been that of J. Stuart Anderson in his *Lawyers and the Making of English Land Law, 1932–1940*.[29] Anderson begins his period of enquiry into the 1925 reforms at an earlier stage when the conflict between the state and the private legal profession over the control of land transfer did not exist. His book is divided into two parts: the first part deals with the period from 1832 to 1875; the second part with the period 1875 to 1940. In the first part, Anderson shows that there emerged during the period under consideration a lawyers' law reform movement which had as its legal culture the supposition that land was to be viewed simply as a form of commercial property to be traded in the open market. From this part, Anderson concludes that during the period under consideration when the reform of land featured in radical politics, the free trade in land became part of the liberals' orthodoxy. From this period emerged the Land Transfer Act of 1897 which was based on a system of title registration and became the forerunner of the subsequent reforming legislation of 1925.

Whichever study one looks at, however, it is clear that the 1925 legislation was only reformist in a legally technical way. Unless Parliament passed new legislation, this one would not be able to deal with the social and moral problems created by deep-seated changes in the latter half of the twentieth century. In its reform, it only reworked the old law on settlements and on trusts of land. The land law of the nineteenth century was plagued with complex settlements and the 1925 legislation was successful in making the transfer of title in these situations more straightforward. There was no definitive statement of property rights (and their incidence) that were to become the concern of owner-occupiers in the twentieth century. Its failing has been commented upon by Murphy and Roberts as follows:

> What sort of animal was the 1925 code? It resembled, in the kind of thing it was, what went before. It was a bundle of

> particulars. The code contained no definitions of dominium, usufructs, servitudes or hypothecs, of the kind familiar to civilians. It was a body of particular rules of a particular kind. They were conveyancing rules. Rules for regulating the transfer of title to land, as well as mostly procedural rules governing legal relationships where land was, to put the matter generally, in 'multiple ownership'. Not that these rules were, or are, unimportant. Generations of lawyers have treated them with the utmost respect, even reverence, because the meat of our law of real property (at least, that part of it which matters to lawyers in their day-to-day activities) is in these rules. The rules are a sort of highway code, the rules of the road telling lawyers how to go about their business, the dos and don'ts of making wills, leases, trusts, of buying and selling houses. Some of the most important rules (in a practical sense) amount to this: if you transfer title to a house to someone, you will be taken to have transferred to that person along with the house this, that and the other (say, the hedges, ditches and fences that are reputed to be part of that piece of land) unless you have expressly stated in your transfer that they are not being transferred. Such provisions are called 'word saving' clauses because that is what they do. They simplify the preparation of the relevant legal instruments. They cut down on the paperwork.[30]

The cardinal feature of the English law of property resides in the distinction between Real Property (realty) and Personal Property (personalty). Yet it is difficult to see why land was not from the beginning of the history of the common law seen as a commodity for doing justice in the community. As Professor J. H. Baker makes it only too clear, 'land is a place to live for man and beast, a source of food and of all other commodities, including – if one has enough to let – money. It outlives its inhabitants, it is immune from destruction by man, and therefore provides a suitably firm base for institutions of government and wealth.'[31]

Perhaps the reason why land did not become a basis for justice was that land and the ownership of land was central to the ideology of the common law which the ruling and landed classes wanted to promote. As Professor E. P. Thompson suggests,

> The law may also be seen as ideology, or as particular rules and sanctions which stand in a definite and active relationship (often a field of conflict) to social norms; and, finally, it may be seen simply in terms of its own logic, rules and procedures – that is, simply *as law*.[32]

The active relationship to which Professor E. P. Thompson refers in a field of conflict is over the right of property and how that may be defined between various competing classes. For much of the history of the common law, that conflict was invariably decided in favour of the landed and ruling classes. The rulers had a need for law, not only to maintain their own hegemony, but also to make the ruled feel that they had a legitimate means to mediate the conflict with the rulers through recourse to the law. This is how the ideology of the law worked:

> What was often at issue was not property, supported by law, against no-property; it was alternative definitions of property rights: for the land owner, enclosure – for the cottager, common rights; for the forest officialdom, 'preserved grounds' for the deer; for the foresters, the right to take turfs. For as long as it remained possible, the ruled – if they could find a purse and a lawyer – would actually fight for their rights by means of law; occasionally the copyholders, resting upon the precedents of sixteenth century law, could actually win a case.[33]

It was the precedents of the sixteenth century which actually became the bane of the common law before the modern jurist and led to its eclipse in the face of the claims of Equity. It was the rigidity of the common law in that period that led to its being challenged from within by its own judges exercising their discretion in individual cases on the basis of parity and equity. The early sixteenth century was the end of the Middle Ages. The common-law courts had become inadequate by this time. In property law, they would not adapt to new claims. The forms of writs were already set out and they restricted the development of new issues and defences. The common-law remedies also gave cause for concern. The courts were content, in a claim for property, if the defendant handed over a sum of money (as if this was a claim for property in chattels or in contract or tort) rather than deliver up the land as required by the plaintiff. In addition, the common-law pleading had become absurd. It focused on one issue to be tried at a time and yet remained engulfed in overwhelming complexity.

When reforms by statute were not forthcoming, individual parties petitioned the King to give them the fair-minded and common-sense redress that was denied them by the common-law courts. These petitions were heard by the Lord Chancellor as the King's highest officer of state. By the sixteenth century, the Chancellor not only gave decisions in his own name but established jurisdiction over freehold land. The jurisdictional basis of the exercise of discretion by the Chancellor (and subsequently by his officers, the Master of the Rolls and the Vice-Chancellors) came to be known as the Court of Chancery. The jurisdiction involved an appeal to the idea of 'conscience' with an emphasis on 'good faith' in the sense of preventing the benefits of an action committed in bad faith. From where did this new jurisdictional basis arise? When these earlier judicial officers were hearing claims they were dealing with private individuals, raising private law claims to protect their private interests. This is exactly what is happening today when private individuals are making frantic attempts to hang on to their homes and residences to protect their property and to stave off homelessness.

In the sixteenth century, the early Chancellors came from an ecclesiastical background and, therefore, when called upon to do justice fell back upon notions of conscience that arose from canon law. They made the pleadings more flexible. Parties were told to do things to an order of court. It was not just enough to deliver up land or to pay sums of money. Thus did the Chancellors lay the basis of the modern law of specific performance of contracts and of injunctions. Where a party fell under accidental hardship or became the victim of oppressive behaviour, the Chancellors offered relief and thereby established a basis for the modern law of the protection of the mortgagor. The right to payment of a debt became a new kind of intangible property that could be created and transferred, and is today known to us as an assignment of a *chose in action*. Their most spectacular creation was, however, the use which is today the basis of the modern trust. Through this clever creation, a person vested with a common-law title to land may nevertheless fall under an obligation to administer it for benefit only of another, who would be his beneficiary. Originally, what arose were 'suits' in the Chancery, and not actions, and the Chancellor would give 'decrees' and not judgments. However, as Jeffrey Hackney suggests, in his lucid account of the development of equity and trusts, 'a combination of repeated circumstance and a desire to treat like cases alike was ultimately to drive the Chancellor into developing a system of rules: equity was to become Equity'.[34]

This is exactly the situation facing the English courts today. They have to do equity. But to what extent can they rely upon the principles of Equity? Are the traditional rules, which were based upon notions of 'good faith' and the avoidance of 'unconscionability' which are derivable from canon law, a sufficient basis for doing justice today, or do the courts have to rethink and redevelop these ideas in a modern setting by an express reference to citizenship ideas, in the form articulated by T. H. Marshall? It would appear that the notions of 'good faith' and 'unconscionability' may not, in themselves, be enough so that the courts would have to respond in a more positive and far-reaching way, taking them beyond the accepted implications of these two terms. We shall see that there is a growing body of evidence that shows that they already do behave in this way. This means that if the courts were to develop their jurisdictional basis further in this manner, they would be doing nothing new. Their actions would be perfectly consistent with their historic and constitutional record in developing the law to meet emerging needs. Their actions, it may even be argued, were far more radical during the period following the sixteenth century than anything that is being suggested in this book along citizenship lines. Yet, the radicalism shown by the courts from the mid-seventeenth century to the early nineteenth century may be an obstacle to the realization of full citizenship rights today unless it can be re-worked along citizenship lines, because that radicalism is presently set into a particular mould. Thus, from about 1530 to 1830 equity was transformed into a systematic body of principles. Its concern was simply to apply principles of private morality to private law transactions between particular parties. Thus, applying the considerations of fair play, the restrictive convenant was transformed from contract to property law. The law of estoppel entered property law and happily acquired itself a home. Express private trusts were allowed to become an instrument for the retention of wealth. These things happened simply because this was what was required by the parties who came to the law. Thus did Equity create a law of Real Property.

Today, the ordinary citizen's needs are more mundane. He may have cause to be concerned about restrictive covenants that affect him or about easements that he may enjoy. However, he is more fundamentally concerned about his right to residential security. To what extent can, or should, the courts protect such rights and upon what principles should they intervene if they decide so to do? Do they do so simply on the basis of principles of 'good faith' and 'unconscionability'? Or, do they do so on the basis of principles that go beyond private morality into a concept of basic citizenship rights? To some societies or groups in society, it may be both socially and morally acceptable for a male spouse to have full ownership of the property. It may even be desirable, according to some. The law may give effect to such a result, and certainly has done in the past. But what is to happen when the exercise of greater and wider citizenship rights by all members of society, women included, leads to a *de facto* exercise of a shared interest of property in the family home? Can the judges continue to do justice, and if so what is their frame of reference? Where a party has not taken steps to safeguard itself, despite the availability of existing rules, can the courts treat vulnerable groups as a specially protected class? As Jeffrey Hackney has observed:

> The judges are facing a dilemma which must be common to all developed legal systems; do we keep to well advertised rules, known to the profession and relied on by them, and, in the interests of system-efficiency and the overall reduction of cost, send away litigants with whom we have considerable personal sympathy, but who have not complied with the rules; or do we never send away deserving litigants without redress, and let the system worry about how the new exception is to fit in, given that all judgments are precedents? This debate ... becomes particularly difficult in times of rapid social change where arrangements made in one period and leading to a clear result in that period, come to be seen to be socially unjust in another. Such times also raise important questions about the legislative functions of the courts in relation to parliament's intentions.[35]

Yet, it is clear that despite these theoretical difficulties the courts cannot sit to administer a law that they know is inequitable in its effect and is bad policy. Even if this is not right, the courts will not long uphold a law that is internally contradictory in terms of its ideology. In the words of Professor E. P. Thompson,

> It is inherent in the especial character of law, as a body of rules and procedures, that it shall apply logical criteria with reference to universality and equity. It is true that certain categories of person may be excluded from this logic (as children or slaves), other categories may be debarred from access to parts of the logic (as women or, for many forms of eighteenth century law, those without certain kinds of property), and that the poor may often be excluded, through penury, from the law's costly procedures. All this, and more, is true. But if too much of this is true, then the consequences are plainly counter-productive. Most men have a strong sense of justice, at least with a regard to their own interests. If the law is evidently partial and unjust then it will mask nothing, legitimise nothing, contribute nothing to any classes' hegemony. The essential precondition for the effectiveness of law, in its function as ideology, is that it shall display an independence from gross manipulation and shall seem to be just. It cannot seem to be so without upholding its own logic and criteria of equity; indeed, on occasion, by actually *being*

> just. And furthermore it is not often the case that a ruling ideology can be dismissed as a mere hypocrisy; even rulers find a need to legitimise their power, to moralise their functions, to feel themselves to be useful and just. In the case of an ancient historical formation like the law, a discipline which requires years of exacting study to master, there will always be some men who actively believe in their own procedures and in the logic of justice. The law may be rhetoric, but it need not be empty rhetoric. Blackstone's *Commentaries* represent an intellectual exercise far more rigorous than could have come from an apologist's pen.[36]

Whatever the reason – and Professor Thompson provides a detailed and erudite account of how law is developed and sustained – the fact is that judges have and do concern themselves with questions of equity and justice. As Jeffrey Hackney notes,

> some judges have also been developing the constructive trust to prevent unconscionable conduct by spreading its net so wide as to catch not only those whom they believe to have been behaving badly, but also those who, while innocent of any personal bad intent are able so to present themselves because they have been taking an unduly carefree approach to wrongdoers with whom they have come into association.[37]

The question is, if judges do concern themselves with these matters, to the extent even of developing legal doctrines, how should they be so concerned? It is suggested that the only equitable basis today is a doctrine of citizenship rights. The doctrine of equity may still be used but its meaning will have to be expanded beyond the confines of private law principles. It is submitted that this is what happened in *Barclays Bank* v. *O'Brien*.[38]

Citizenship as a New Equity in the Modern Law

In *Barclays Bank plc* v. *O'Brien*, more than a decade and a half after *Boland*, the House of Lords revisited the thorny question of the conflictual claims of social rights and interests *vis-à-vis* legal rights. It is important to understand the context in which the House of Lords was called upon to mediate this conflict. The economic recession of the late 1980s had led to a dramatic rise in the number of mortgage repossession actions.[39] From the beginning of the recession in 1989 when the annual figure of repossession actions was 53,066, the numbers more than doubled to 142,905 at the peak of the recession in 1991. Thereafter the number of such actions by lending institutions began to come down, but still stood at 105,283 in 1993.[40] In the *O'Brien* case, the House of Lords was looking at the situation of a wife who becomes a surety for her husband's debt to a third-party creditor and embarked upon an analysis of how equity can resolve such a situation. In *O'Brien* the husband had been unable to keep up his mortgage repayments and the wife was threatened with homelessness on account of his default.

The House of Lords found an answer outside the legal provisions in a way that was even more radical than its decision in *Boland*. It is true that the House of Lords focused on the constructive knowledge of the bank of the misrepresentation by the husband to his wife, of the reason for which he was taking a second charge on the matrimonial property and the undue influence that he thereby exercised, and the bank's failure to take reasonable steps to avoid being fixed with such constructive knowledge. However, the long-term effects of the House of Lords judgment are far-reaching, as will be seen below, and cannot be overlooked. Yet, it is difficult to see how else the court could have reached an ethically and socially satisfying and satisfactory result. The device that their Lordships used was the time-honoured one of the equitable jurisdiction in the court to do justice when the formal provisions of the law can no longer provide an adequate answer. Arguably, this shows that what is radical at first sight is not so on a closer examination of the judicial process. It is well known that the property legislation of 1925 is ill fitted to deal with questions of social justice.[41]

The House of Lords heard joint appeals in two cases on the same day in *Barclays Bank* v. *O'Brien*[42] and *CIBC Mortgages plc* v. *Pitt*.[43] The question that was common to both appeals was this: when will equity protect a wife who becomes a surety for her husband's debt to a third-party creditor? In both cases, the wives had been induced by wrongful conduct, through either misrepresentation or undue influence, to charge their matrimonial home, as a security for their husbands' financial interests. In the first case, the wife won. In the second case, she lost. The crucial difference lay in the fact that in the first case the wife did not stand to gain financially herself but in the second case she did. Mrs O'Brien had charged the matrimonial home to the bank for overdraft facilities in order to extend her husband's business in which she had no interest. Mrs Pitt charged her home in order to secure a loan that was made both to Mr and Mrs Pitt jointly for the express purpose of discharging a first mortgage over their home and buying a holiday home for their joint use.

The House of Lords was confronted by the Privy Council decision in *Turnbull and Co.* v. *Duval*[44] on which the modern law was founded. This was a turn of the century case where a security granted by a wife for her husband's business debts was held by Lord Lindley to be unenforceable because the creditor had not taken any steps to recognize the existence of the wife. However, the equitable principle that the Privy Council applied was left unclear. Lord Lindley's decision in *Turnbull*,[45] however, did lead to the development of two separate judicial approaches in the law on this subject. Where the husband was regarded as the creditor's agent in procuring the wife's consent to the proposed security, there the husband's wrongdoing was imputed to the creditor. This gave rise to the 'agency theory'.[46]

Several Court of Appeal decisions reflect the agency theory. Where the debtor and the surety were in such a relationship that influence over the surety by the debtor and reliance by the surety was a natural and probable feature of the relationship, there the surety would be deemed to be a member of a 'protected class'. This was the 'special equity theory',[47] offering special protection to wives who provided a security for their husbands' debts, and its most erudite exposition took place in the *O'Brien* case by Scott LJ in the Court of Appeal. Those who fell into this protected class could not have their surety obligations enforced against them if three conditions were satisfied. First, if the creditor was aware of the likelihood of influence between the debtor and the surety; second, if the debtor had obtained the surety's consent by the undue influence or misrepresentation or without 'an adequate understanding of the nature and effect of the transaction'; and third, if the creditor failed to take reasonable steps to make sure that the surety had given a true and informed consent to the transaction. According to Scott LJ in the Court of Appeal, if a wife failed to understand the transaction for which she was providing a surety, this could provide a clear basis for relief.[48] By the time that the House of Lords came to look at these issues, there were not only two separate approaches for deciding when creditors became responsible for either the misunderstanding or the private pressure inflicted on a wife by her husband, but also considerable uncertainty about which approach would apply when.

In the House of Lords, Lord Browne-Wilkinson gave the only speech for the unanimous rulings on behalf of their Lordships. He held that the present law was based upon 'obscure and possibly mistaken foundations' and purported to 'restate the law in a form in which it is principled, reflects the current requirements of society, and provides as much certainty as possible'.[49] His Lordship accepted the 'agency theory' but rejected the 'special equity theory'. The answer lay always in the ordinary principles of equity. Where the husband was acting as the third party's agent, or the third party had notice, whether actual or constructive, of the facts giving rise to the wife's equity, the wife could set aside the transaction. Where, however, a wife had merely failed to understand the transaction, creditors could not be required to prove that the wife had understood it, as contended for by Scott LJ on the basis of the 'special equity theory'. Instead, their Lordships would apply the doctrine of notice from equity. This was the approach taken by Peter Gibson LJ in the Court of Appeal in *Pitt*.[50] This, in their Lordships' view, would avoid any injustice to the wife. Therefore, where the creditor had actual or constructive notice of the wife's consent to providing security as having been obtained in consequence of a legal wrong committed by her husband, there the security would be voidable. If the transaction was not on its face to the financial advantage of the wife then creditors will be fixed with constructive notice if the relationship between the borrower and the security provider is one involving a substantial risk to the security provider. Provided that creditors then took 'reasonable steps' to insist that the wife attend a private meeting to be told of the extent of her liability as a surety and to be warned of the risk that she was running, as well as be told of the desirability of her taking independent legal advice, the creditor would be beyond reproach.[51]

Their Lordships did not, however, rule out 'exceptional cases' where a creditor had knowledge of further facts which would render the presence of undue influence not only possible but also probable and in such a case the wife would have to be separately advised.[52] This approach was taken by the House of Lords in express recognition of the law's 'tender treatment' of married women. Lord Browne-Wilkinson recognized that this

> is due to the fact that, even today, many wives repose confidence and trust in their husbands in relation to their financial affairs. This tenderness of the law is reflected by the fact that voluntary dispositions by the wife in favour of her husband are more likely to be set aside than other dispositions . . . Moreover the informality of business dealings between spouses *raises a substantial risk* that the husband has not accurately stated to the wife the nature of the liability she is undertaking . . . [53] (Emphasis added.)

As a statement of law, this is impeccably well stated. In strict doctrinal terms the judgment of the House of Lords is compelling. It allows the House of Lords to protect the interests of vulnerable wives on the basis of well-established equitable principles. But does it afford enough protection and does it provide the *kind* of protection to property rights that all citizens today can reasonably come to expect?

It is submitted that judgment of the House of Lords did not go far enough in securing basic citizenship rights to property because it was based upon the traditional grounds of equity that were not entirely accommodating for the needs of modern society. While the case of *Williams & Glyn's Bank* v. *Boland* in the House of Lords had brought to the forefront the scenario of wives providing security for their husbands' debts, recent years have seen an increase in both attempts by wives to avoid liability, and attempts by bankers to establish procedures that would allow them to enforce securities. Whatever legal principle was to be used by the court, it had to address the fact that owner-occupation had risen dramatically since the Second World War, small businesses had been encouraged by the government since the 1980s, and spouses had joint legal title to the family home invariably. Yet, the equality between the parties is only superficial. Most wives, as the House of Lords recognized, will follow their husbands' advice on business matters without independent thought. An emotionally dependent wife may be especially vulnerable to pressure from her husband to give consent to business transactions with which she does not necessarily agree. The House of Lords' judgment certainly recognized the current changes in social and cultural behaviour, and the judgment sought to give protection not only to wives, but also to other co-habitants as well, whether homosexual or heterosexual, who had reposed financial trust and confidence in a principal debtor. However, the House of Lords did not follow through the practical effects on a day-to-day basis of a private dependency of one spouse on another. How does emotional dependency that is private translate into a financial vulnerability that is public? And, is the classical doctrine of equity an appropriate means for dealing with this problem?

To answer this, let us consider the two decisions in *O'Brien* and *Pitt*. The particularly notable feature in both cases is that the creditor did not act *mala fide*. In fact, as Lord Browne-Wilkinson recognized:

> Given that there are two *innocent* parties, each enjoying rights, the earlier right prevails against the latter right if the acquirer of the latter right knows of the earlier right (actual notice) or would have discovered it had he taken proper steps (constructive notice).[54]

In both these cases, therefore, the major difficulty arose from the fact that there was an absence of fraud on the part of the creditor, an absence of any inducement of the undue influence on the part of the chargee, and an absence of actual knowledge on the part of the creditor. Given this, it was surely unusual to invoke the equitable jurisdiction of the court since there was no 'good faith' to maintain and no 'unconscionability' to avoid. Indeed, in *O'Brien* the bank manager gave express instructions to his subordinates that the husband and wife should be made aware of the nature and effect of the documents they were signing and should take independent legal advice if they were in doubt. However, those instructions were not followed by the bank staff responsible for arranging for the husband and wife to sign the documents. The husband signed the documents without reading them and the next day took his wife to the bank and she also signed the documents without reading them. Yet, the judgment of the House of Lords suggests that a wronged wife, having granted a charge to a creditor, will still have an equitable right to avoid the transaction which takes priority over the creditor's charge on the grounds that the creditor has constructive notice. This is a radical doctrine which is not explicable in strict equitable terms. Yet this did not assist Mrs Pitt, who was, by all accounts, in a far more vulnerable position than Mrs O'Brien.

This suggests that the application of the equitable doctrine in this situation is not only theoretically unconvincing but practically unhelpful. Had the decision been based on a wider idea of citizenship rights and the right to property as being integral to those citizenship rights, Mrs Pitt, who was at least just as deserving, would have fared as well as Mrs O'Brien. Her husband told her that he would like to borrow some money on the security of the house and to use the loan to buy shares on the stockmarket. Mrs Pitt was clearly unhappy with this but had to agree because of the pressure from her husband. The husband and wife then together signed an application form for a loan from the plaintiff mortgage company of £150,000 for a period of twenty years, the purpose of the loan being expressly to pay off the existing mortgage and purchase a holiday home. The plaintiff agreed to advance the £150,000 for nineteen years and both husband and wife signed the mortgage offer and legal charge. However, Mrs Pitt did not read those documents before signing them nor did she receive separate advice about the transaction and neither did anyone suggest that she should do so. She did not know the amount that was being borrowed. Lord Browne-Wilkinson was bound to overlook all of this if he was to view the situation through the lens of the doctrine of notice. He asked what was known to the creditor 'that could *put it on enquiry* so as to fix it with constructive notice?' He found:

> So far as the (creditor) was aware, the transaction consisted of a joint loan to the husband and wife to finance the discharge of an existing mortgage on (the family home), and as to the balance to be applied in buying a holiday home. The loan was

> advanced to both husband and wife jointly. There was nothing to indicate to the (creditor) that this was anything other than a normal advance to husband and wife for their joint benefit.[55]

The reason why Mrs Pitt could not win, as Mrs O'Brien had done, was quite simply as follows:

> What distinguishes the case of the *joint advance* from the *surety case* is that, in the latter, there is not only the possibility of undue influence having been exercised but also the *increased risk* of it having in fact been exercised because, *at least on its face*, the guarantee by a wife of her husband's debts is *not for her financial benefit*. It is the combination of these two factors that puts the creditor on enquiry.[56] (Emphases added.)

It would surely have been far more conducive to justice to have adopted the format of Scott LJ in the Court of Appeal in *O'Brien* and to apply a formulation of the 'special equity theory' to afford special protection to wives in this situation than to have been preoccupied with the preservation and application of a theoretical doctrine that was ill-fitted to the facts. It was ill-fitted for two reasons.

Firstly, the judgment of their Lordships is open to the theoretical objection that it falls foul of the statutory provisions in relation to registered land. Section 20(1) and Section 59(6) of the Land Registration Act 1925 removed the doctrine of notice and made it irrelevant in relation to registered land.[57] The matter was clearly put in the *Boland* case by Lord Wilberforce when he declared that 'the system is designed to free the purchaser from the hazards of notice – real or constructive – which, in the case of unregistered land, involved him in enquiries, often quite elaborate, failing which he might be bound by equities.[58] Under the statutory provisions both actual and constructive notice were removed. The only exception was in cases of fraud, and, of course, in *O'Brien* and *Pitt* there was no fraud. Their Lordships' judgment is also contrary to Section 2 of the Law of Property Act 1925 which states that a chargee's interest 'shall overreach any equitable interest affecting that state whether or not he has notice thereof'. This means that providing that an equitable interest is, at the date of the conveyance, 'capable of being overreached, it shall be overreached provided that the statutory requirement for the payment of capital money to two trustees for the sale has been complied with'. It is well known that 'commercial' equitable rights which are duly protected by registration cannot be overreached, but that 'family' equitable interests can be overreached. The net result is that if payment is made to the husband and wife then this would have the effect of overreaching the wife's equity regardless of constructive notice.

Secondly, the judgment of their Lordships is open to objection on practical grounds because Mrs Pitt was in a far more vulnerable and invidious position than Mrs O'Brien. Mrs Pitt, unlike Mrs O'Brien, had no control over the form in which the transaction was going to take place or the capacity in which she was going to be involved. Mrs O'Brien knew that she was signing a mortgage of the matrimonial home but believed that the security was limited to £60,000 and would last only three weeks, which was not true, because the situation had been misrepresented to her by her husband. In contrast, Mrs Pitt not only had no control over her family expenditure but was clearly subjected to grave emotional pressure in entering this transaction. In short, she was under duress. Her vulnerability and lack of control over family expenditure is plain from the decision of Peter Gibson LJ in the Court of Appeal when he recorded that

> Mr Pitt paid most of the bills and gave Mrs Pitt money for housekeeping and other expenditure such as a new coat. Mr Pitt chose the furniture, fittings, wallpaper and holiday destinations ... (Mrs Pitt's) evidence was that in relation to big items of expenditure *there was usually an argument*, she would be *shouted down* and told it was *in their best interests*, and that she would also be told that she was stupid and she did not know what she was talking about.[59] (Emphases added.)

Mrs Pitt's helplessness and condition of duress is evident from the decision of the Trial Judge, Recorder D. T. A. Davies, when he noted that Mrs Pitt

> went on to say that if she had refused to co-operate *her life would have become a nightmare*. He would have gone on about it and continually *worn her down* ... he would say how silly she was, and this sort of thing and *just would not stop*. She had accepted that he had mentioned that their standard of living would be improved, but *freedom from being pestered was more important than that*. As she said: 'I would rather have a peaceful life than a lot of money.'[60] (Emphases added.)

In these circumstances, it is quite unrealistic and artificial for their Lordships to resolve the situation on the basis of what appeared to be the case on the 'face of the transaction'. The fact is, that notwithstanding the commercial assessment of the likely benefits to the respective wives in *O'Brien* and *Pitt*, the court knew that Mrs Pitt had entered this transaction contrary to her will. The court also knew (and had gone to great lengths to record as much) that even today many wives repose confidence and trust in their husbands, in relation to their financial affairs. That being so, it simply did not make sense to conclude that: 'If third parties were to be fixed with constructive notice of undue influence in relation to every transaction between husband and wife, *such transactions would become almost impossible.*'[61] (Emphasis added.)

This is a far cry from Lord Denning who, as we have earlier seen, recorded in the *Birkom Investments* case that 'I prefer to see that justice is done; and let the conveyancers look after themselves'.[62] The Lords' answer to the existence of private pressure and misunderstanding on the part of the wife is simply to stipulate that creditors be obliged to increase the information that they provide to wives. However, all that this will do is to avoid misrepresentations in a case like *O'Brien*. It will not avoid undue emotional pressure of a private kind by a husband on a wife. It is unhelpful to resort to the classical doctrine of equity in this case. If the courts were to think in terms of wider citizenship rights for all members of the community and an obligation on the part of corporate bodies to protect those rights, it could simply have stipulated that there should be a legal obligation on the part of lending institutions to provide separate legal advice to a wife in all situations, whether that of a surety for the debts of a husband or of a joint loan. If the 'tender treatment' of married women in the law is to be real then this must be a basic minimum. Wives can be expressly told that their home is at risk unless the payments are kept up, an explanation of the past, present and future prognosis of the husband's financial situation, a blunt statement to the wife that she will gain nothing personally but risk her home, and an express advice that being loyal to her husband does not mean that she is under compulsion to sign the charge. Banks and building societies will not stop transacting just because they have to give this advice.

The Lords' failure to stipulate a requirement of express separate legal advice in this way has resulted in a number of cases being unjustly decided against wives since *O'Brien* and *Pitt*. In *Massey* v. *Midland Bank plc*,[63] Miss Massey granted a second charge on her home to Midland Bank to secure an overdraft to a limit that she wrongly thought was £40,000, for the benefit of her long-time lover, Mr Potts. Potts had deceived Miss Massey about the business's future prospects. The Midland Bank required Miss Massey to be independently advised but, crucially, did not provide this advice itself. Instead, Miss Massey was advised by Mr Potts' own solicitors who asked Miss Massey no questions and gave her no advice about the financial standing of Mr Potts' company. At first instance it was held that Mr Potts' solicitor was not the agent of the creditor bank so Miss Massey could not have the charge avoided. On appeal to the Court of

Appeal, Steyn LJ applied *O'Brien* and held, firstly, that the transaction was not on its face to Miss Massey's financial advantage; and secondly, that there was substantial risk that in procuring her to act as surety, Mr Potts had committed a legal or equitable wrong that entitled her to have the transaction set aside. However, the bank had taken reasonable steps to insure that her agreement to the charge was properly obtained. Steyn LJ said of Mr Potts' solicitor, who advised Miss Massey, that 'how far a solicitor should go in probing the matter, and giving advice, is a matter for the solicitor's professional judgment and a matter between him and his client. The Bank is not generally involved in the nature and extent of the solicitor's advice.' However, this is precisely the objection with this sort of practice. If the bank had specifically involved itself in ensuring equity and parity between all respective parties in a transaction, Miss Massey would not have been liable on the charge. Mr Potts had chosen his own solicitors to give his co-habitee advice on the charge and the Bank did not know what was said at the interview and had been under no duty to enquire.

In *Banco Exterior Internacional* v. *Mann*[64] a trial judge tried to look at the situation from the viewpoint of the wife but was reversed on appeal by the Court of Appeal, applying *Massey*. This case well illustrates how complex and dangerously risky the situation can be for the wife unless the bank ensures advice that is not only separate but seen to be separate. In this case the bank loaned £175,000 to a company owned by Mr Mann on the security of a second mortgage over the jointly occupied matrimonial home which was in the husband's, Mr Mann's, sole name. The bank required that the nature of the charge should be explained to Mr Mann's wife by a solicitor and that the solicitor should certify that this had been done. The solicitor for the husband's company gave such advice partly in the presence of the husband. The solicitor then issued a certificate of due explanation to the bank. The judge at first instance refused the bank's claim to enforce security against Mrs Mann on the grounds that it had not taken reasonable steps to avoid being fixed with constructive notice of her rights. This was despite the fact that the solicitor had written separately to Mrs Mann to say that she could not set up any claim to ownership in the house which would defeat the bank's interest. The judge at first instance held, however, that the possibility that the solicitor might be the solicitor for the company had not been excluded. The solicitor could not be regarded as being independent of Mrs Mann's husband. Therefore, a mere understanding on her part was not enough if she thought that she had no choice in the matter. Had there been independent advice, she might well have thought that she had such a choice.

On further appeal, however, Morritt LJ refused to consider this situation from the viewpoint of the wife. The true question in his view, in giving the majority decision of the court, was not how Mrs Mann regarded the transaction but how it appeared to the bank and whether the bank had taken reasonable steps. The bank was entitled to rely on the fact that a solicitor had undertaken the task and that he was sufficiently independent. The solicitor could have declined if he felt a conflict of interest. The bank could assume that the effect of the declaration, signed by Mrs Mann, would make clear to her the risks arising from default. The bank could reasonably and justifiably assume that the solicitor would appreciate why his advice and warranty was being sought in these circumstances. With this majority judgment Sir Thomas Bingham MR agreed, but Hobhouse LJ dissented.

In the latter's judgment, *O'Brien* had well and clearly stated that 'the wife or other chargor must attend a private meeting in the absence of the husband with a representative of the creditor at which she is told the extent of her liability as surety, warned of the risk she is running and urged to take independent advice'. Hobhouse LJ observed that the bank had not advised Mrs Mann to take independent advice and she had never received any independent advice. The bank could not have been unaware that Mrs Mann might sign under her husband's undue influence and this is indeed what had happened. Therefore, the advice that had to be independently and separately given in this matter would have to be general business and pastoral advice. In the express words of Hobhouse LJ, 'it may be necessary for the solicitor to say to the wife: "I know that you felt that you have no option but to sign, but you are wrong. You do have a choice and I must advise you that it is not in your best interests to sign this document. You should feel under no obligation to do so. You are asking for my advice. My advice to you is: do not sign."'[65]

It may be argued that there are dangers in this approach and that a solicitor is not competent to advise on the general wisdom of signing or not signing unless he has detailed knowledge of the precise circumstances of a transaction. However, it has to be remembered that a wife who is under duress is not competent either. She is turning to the solicitor precisely so that she can be objectively advised on these matters. Solicitors, moreover, are the best people to give such advice and, traditionally, would have given such advice, where it was needed. Of course, the best practice must, as Steyn LJ said in *Massey*, 'strike a fair balance between the need to protect wives (and others in a like position) . . . and the need to avoid unnecessary impediments to using the matrimonial home as a security'. However, a private meeting with the surety, advising the surety of the right to independent advice, would appear to be the minimum if continuing difficulties are to be avoided.

In *Bank of Baroda* v. *Rayarel*[66] a wife provided security for her husband's loan by charging her interest in the matrimonial home. She was given advice by the bank's solicitor dealing with the loan. She signed that she had been advised of the effect of the charge and of her right to independent advice and the solicitor of the bank countersigned the declaration. The Court of Appeal held that the wife was bound. Hoffmann LJ said that the bank's legal department 'was not required to commit the professional discourtesy of doubting whether the solicitor had actually given the required advice nor was it required to inform the solicitor of his professional duties'. Hirst LJ held that any questioning of the correctness of the certificate would have involved questioning the probity and honesty of the solicitor, which the bank was not required to do.

In another case, *Midland Bank plc* v. *Serter*,[67] the refusal to question a bank's solicitor, who may well be acting for both parties and who may well be in a conflict of interest situation, was taken to new heights. Here the bank's solicitor acted for the lending bank as well as the husband in a loan secured on the matrimonial home which was in joint names. The bank's solicitor explained the nature of the loan to the wife by telephone and the husband subsequently obtained her signature. Before the Court of Appeal the question arose whether the bank had constructive notice of the husband's undue influence. It was held that the bank's solicitor was the agent of the bank only for the purposes of registering the security. When the bank's solicitor advised the wife he either acted for her or was acting for her husband. What the bank's solicitor knew could not be imputed to the bank. If the bank's solicitor had knowledge of the husband's undue influence on his wife the bank could not be said to have had constructive notice of this. Consequently when the husband defaulted on his payments the bank could enforce the security against the wife. If this is right, then it surely nullifies the effect of *O'Brien*. It negates any idea of a 'tender treatment' in the law for married women. Most importantly, it shows that protection of basic rights is not achievable through the application of the court's equitable doctrine, but rather, should have been predicated upon a more general doctrine of the rights of citizens.

That *O'Brien* will not bring wide-ranging change to the rights of vulnerable persons, who stand surety or are made to stand as surety for a principal debtor, is evident from the judgment of Nourse LJ in the Court of Appeal, in the case of *T.S.B. Bank* v. *Camfield*[68] when he said that

> while the House of Lords in *O'Brien* might have extended the application of the doctrine of constructive notice to transactions to which it had not previously held to apply, the consequences of that application had to be the same as those which followed in any other case where a third party was affected by notice, actual, constructive or imputed, as of another's right.

All that is required, it seems, of a lending institution is that it has had no notice of another's right. It is then possible for it to deprive another of their proprietary rights.

Louis D. Brandeis, who sat on the US Supreme Court from 1916 to 1939, developed a theory of lawyering that emphasized morality and a knowledge of real life circumstances that went beyond simply a knowledge of law. To be able to give accurate and appropriate advice lawyers had to acquaint themselves with all the facts, including the social facts. They then had to give fearless and independent advice. In an early memorandum in his handwriting, entitled 'The practice of the law', he states as follows:

> Broad Scope of Opportunity . . . Question – how a man handles it . . . Broad interests . . . Thoroughness in law – Know not only specific Q. But whole subject. Can't otherwise know the facts. Know thoroughly each fact. Don't believe client witness – examine documents. Draw on the imagination. Know the whole subject. Know about persons . . . Persistency – Courage. Devotion. You may become master. Don't have personal interest. Advise client what he should have – Not what he wants . . . Know not only those facts which bear on Direct controversy. But know all facts that Surround.[69]

Brandeis's vision of the ideal lawyer was one who was free and independent and not one who became the servant of corporations. Such lawyers confine themselves to a knowledge of nothing more than their client's wishes. Worse, they bargain away their freedom in exchange for large salaries and hurt society in the process. In his speech 'The living law'[70] he charged many lawyers of becoming hired hands for the ever-growing corporations that became hallmarks of the twentieth century. In a speech to the Harvard Ethical Society in 1905 entitled 'The opportunity in the law' he reminded his audience that, in earlier years, 'nearly every great lawyer was . . . a statesman; and nearly every statesman, great or small, was a lawyer'. Now, he regretted, lawyers no longer held 'a position of independence, between the wealthy and the people, prepared to curb the excesses of either'. In his opinion too many lawyers had turned their backs on the people in order 'to become adjuncts of great corporations'.[71]

It is easy to deal with these criticisms. A lawyer for the lending bank or the debtor husband who also decides to advise a surety wife is ostensibly providing a public interest service to that wife. Brandeis himself is a paradigm for today's public interest lawyers. These are lawyers who voluntarily assume responsibility for representing the people when they are confronted by large, wealthy and sometimes capricious institutions, be they private or public. If lawyers chose to be engaged in such a service then the courts should insist on such a service being meticulously performed. Citizenship values demand nothing less. It is not enough to say: trust the lawyer.

Conclusion

In this chapter we have seen some very clear cases of law in which the courts can play a pivotal role in shoring up delicate property interests that stand threatened if contractual obligations are to be strictly enforced. These cases are clear examples of citizenship concerns shown by the courts based on the recognition of an implied egalitarian social contract between mortgagors and mortgagees and even beyond to innocent third parties. There are unmistakable echoes in *O'Brien* of what was said a decade earlier in *Boland*. Lord Denning in the latter case declared that 'Anyone who lends money on the security of a matrimonial home nowadays ought to realise that the wife may have a share in it. He ought to make sure that the wife agrees to it . . . .' And Lord Wilberforce in the House of Lords said that 'What is involved is a departure from an easygoing practice of dispensing with enquiries as to occupation beyond that of the vendor and accepting the risks of doing so'. Lord Scarman simply held that 'bankers and solicitors exist to provide the service that the public needs'. This is a citizen-orientated view, explicable in fundamentally citizenship terms, that is echoed by Lord Browne-Wilkinson in *O'Brien* when he declares that 'the informality of business dealings between spouses raises a substantial risk that the husband has not accurately stated for the wife the nature of the liability she is undertaking . . . '. There is, however, no room for complacency, for it is regrettable that in *Pitt* an impractical distinction is drawn between a joint advance and a surety case, leading to gross injustice for the wife. And in *Banco Exterior*, Hobhouse LJ is a lone dissenting voice championing the spirit of *Boland* when he declares that solicitors, providing a service to the public, should take it upon themselves to say positively that 'It is not in your best interests to sign this document' and that 'My advice to you is: do not sign'. It is clear that there is not yet in place a coherent judicial policy of promoting parity and equity between mortgagees and mortgagors and their families.

Notes and References

1 *Kovacs* v. *Cooper*, 336 U.S. 77, 95 (1949) (concurring opinion).

2 Pollock and Maitland, F. W. (1968 edn) *The History of English Law* (2), p. 406. London.

3 [1981] AC 487.

4 [1994] AC 180.

5 *Supra*, note 3.

6 The system that was set up under the Land Registration Act 1925 was designed to discard reliance on title deeds by requiring all interests to be registered, thus removing the need for a repeated examination of the same title. The system registers titles, but does not register land. A prospective purchaser need only examine the register to see if the vendor has the right to sell, and if any third party interests affect the land to be sold. The Land Register is kept under the control of the Chief Land Registrar at the Land Registry in London and in 19 District Land Registries. The Register is divided up into the 'Property Register' (describing the land by reference to a plan); the 'Proprietorship Register' (which includes the name and address of the Registered Proprietor of the stated title); and the 'Charges Register' (which contains notices and entries that adversely affect the land). There are four categories of interest that may be registered. These are (i) registerable interests; (ii) registered interests; (iii) minor interests; and (iv) overriding interests. The registerable interests are interests that are capable of substantive registration in their own right and produce separate titles, each with its own individual register. The classes of title under which registerable interests may be described are absolute title, qualified title, possessory title and good leasehold title. The minor interests are defined in s. 3(xv) of the LRA 1925 as 'interests not capable of being disposed of or created by registered dispositions and capable of being overridden . . . by the proprietors unless protected as provided by this Act . . . '. This means that minor interests constitute a residual category which consists of all interests in registered land which are not registerable interests, registered charges and overriding interests. The important thing to recognize in registered land is that all interests have to be registered if they are to have legal efficacy. Anything not registered does not count, unless it is an overriding interest. Overriding interests are described in s. 70 of the LRA 1925. Minor interests may be registered and protected by entering a notice, a restriction, a caution, or an inhibition.

7 Overriding interests are defined in the LRA 1925 as 'all encumbrances, interests, rights and powers not entered on the register but subject to which registered dispositions are . . . to take effect' (see s. 3(xvi)). Under s. 70(1) there is a list of overriding interests which include easements not being equitable easements required to be protected by notice on the register, rights acquired or in the course of being acquired under the Limitation Acts, rights of persons in actual occupation of the land and leases granted for a term not exceeding 21 years.

8 [1957] Ch. 475.

9 [1971] Ch. 892.

10 [1978] 26 P & CR 448, at p. 454.
11 [1979] Ch. 312, p. 343 (per Browne LJ).
12 [1981] AC 487, at p. 502F.
13 [1979] Ch. 312, p. 332.
14 *Loc. cit.*
15 *Loc. cit.*
16 [1979] QP 467, p. 484.
17 [1979] Ch. 312, pp. 332–3.
18 [1979] Ch. 312, p. 339.
19 *Supra*, note 3, at p. 508H.
20 *Supra*, note 3, at p. 510B–C.
21 *Ibid.*, at A–B.
22 A classic statement of the doctrine of conversion appears in the judgment of Cross LJ in *Irani Finance Limited* v. *Singh* [1971] Ch. 59, p. 79, where he suggests that the whole purpose of the trust for sale is to enable third party purchasers to buy land free from beneficial encumbrances through the equitable doctrine of conversion: 'to hold these to be equitable interests in the land itself would be to frustrate this purpose.'
23 [1979] Ch. 312, p. 329.
24 [1979] Ch. 312, p. 336.
25 *Supra*, note 3, at p. 507F.
26 *Supra*, note 3, at p. 510G.
27 Offer, Avner (1977) The origin of the Law of Property Acts 1910–1925. *Modern Law Review* (40) p. 505.
28 Offer, Avner (1981) *Property and Politics 1870–1914*. Cambridge.
29 Anderson, J. Stuart (1992) *Lawyers and the Making of English Land Law, 1832–1940*. Oxford.
30 Murphy, W. T. and Roberts, Simon (1987) *Understanding Property Law*, pp. 171–2. London.
31 Baker, John H. (1990) *An Introduction to Legal History*, p. 255. London.
32 Thompson, E. P. (1990) *Whigs and Hunters*, p. 260. London.
33 *Ibid.*, p. 261.
34 Hackney, Jeffrey (1987) *Understanding Equity and Trusts*, p. 18. London.
35 *Ibid.*, p. 39.
36 Thompson, E. P. (1990) *Whigs and Hunters*, p. 263. London.
37 Hackney, Jeffrey (1987) *Understanding Equity and Trusts*, p. 40. London. The current chapter demonstrates many examples of this.
38 [1994] AC 180.
39 See Boseley, Sarah (1995) Going cheap: the repossessed stuff of broken dreams. *Guardian*, Friday 2 June.
40 Thompson, Michael P. (1995) A very wide discretion? *The Conveyancer* (pp. 51–6), p. 51.
41 For example, Murphy and Roberts conclude that 'the categories of English land law have ceased in large measure to mirror social relations in the way they once did': Murphy and Roberts, *op. cit.*, p. 196.
42 [1994] AC 180.
43 [1994] AC 200.
44 [1902] AC 429 (PC).

45 *Ibid.*, p. 435.

46 *Kingsnorth Trust Limited* v. *Bell* [1986] 1 WLR 119 (CA), p. 123 (per Lindley LJ); *Midland Bank plc* v. *Perry* [1988] 56 P & CR 202 (CA); *Lloyds Bank plc* v. *Egremont* [1990] 2 FLR 351 (CA); and *Bank of Credit and Commerce SA* v. *Oboody* [1990] 1 QB 923 (CA) which comprise the leading cases.

47 See the earlier decision of Dixon J in *Yerkey* v. *Jones* [1939] 63 CLR 649, although some support for this view also comes from the earlier case of *Chaplin and Co. Limited* v. *Brammall* [1908] 1 KB 233 (CA). The most recent cases supporting this view include *Kingsnorth Trust Limited* v. *Bell* [1986] 1 WLR 119 (CA), and *Barclays Bank plc* v. *Kennedy* [1989] 1 FLR 356 (CA).

48 *Supra*, note 42, at p. 187.

49 *Supra*, note 42, at p. 194H (also note observation at p. 185H).

50 *Supra*, note 43, at pp. 210–11.

51 *Supra*, note 42, at p. 197A–B.

52 *Supra*, note 42, at p. 196B–C.

53 *Loc. cit.*, at D.

54 *Supra*, note 42, at p. 195G–H.

55 *Supra*, note 43, at p. 211C–D.

56 *Loc. cit.*

57 Under s. 20(1) a disposition for valuable consideration of a legal estate in registered land confers the estate upon the transferee subject only to 'the incumberances and other entries, if any, appearing on the register . . . and . . . to the overriding interests . . . '. The estate transferred or created is in consequence 'free from all other estates and interests whatsoever . . . '. Under s. 59(6) this position is made even more clear because 'a purchaser acquiring title under a registered disposition shall not be concerned with any . . . document, matter, or claim (not being an overriding interest . . .) which is not protected by a caution, or other entry on the register, whether he has or has not notice thereof, express, implied, or constructive'.

58 [1981] AC 487, p. 503.

59 See *The Times*, 7 April 1993.

60 Quoted from Fehlberg, Belinda (1994) The husband, the bank, the wife and her signature. *Modern Law Review* (57) (pp. 467–75), p. 473.

61 *Supra*, note 43, at p. 211E.

62 [1979] QB 467, p. 484.

63 [1995] 1 All ER 929. See also the quote at (1995) *The Conveyancer*, p. 148.

64 [1995] 1 All ER 936.

65 [1995] 1 All ER 951.

66 *The Times*, 19 January 1995.

67 [1995] EGCS 38, [1995] 3 CL 387.

68 [1995] 1 All ER 951.

69 See Strum, Philippa (1995) *Brandeis on Democracy*, p. 6. Kansas.

70 *Ibid.*, pp. 59–66.

71 *Ibid.*, pp. 52–9.

3

Bankruptcy and Insolvency

There is nothing which so generally strikes the imagination, and engages the affections of mankind, as the right of property; or that the sole and despotic dominium which one man claims and exercises over the external things of the world, in total exclusion of the right of any other individual in the universe . . .
Sir William Blackstone

Central to the idea of democratic citizenship is the right in property matters *not to be excluded* from one's property. As Professor C. B. Macpherson observed,

> democratic pressures on those governments which uphold capitalist property rights are becoming strong enough that any such government which also claims to be furthering a democratic society . . . will have to acknowledge that property as a right of access . . . must be increasingly an individual right not to be excluded from access.[1]

Before the advent of capitalist society, indeed, people had a wider access to common property. Capitalism led to exclusionary rights. Feudal and pre-capitalist society, being based on a link with the land which might be the land around the village or the manor or the land in the woods or the river flowing by, recognized the right in those people associated with the land to benefit from and exploit it in common with other individuals who were similarly entitled. This was not just a public right of access to common land but it also had important personal proprietary attributes. There were rights that prevented others from excluding oneself from the benefit of resources upon which one was dependent for one's livelihood.

After the rise of capitalism in the seventeenth century, however, land could be commercially exploited and exchanged and property became freely alienable. Property was capital whose value depended upon its marketability. It was not any longer a simple revenue right in the land. There occurred, as Professor Roger Cotterrell recognizes, 'the unfettered employment of property assets as capital' so that rather than right holders laying claim to the right in the land it was the land itself that became transferable in the market: 'the thing itself became, in common parlance, the property.'[2] Capitalist market economy also required the privatization of common property in order to enable effective resource allocation to take place in the full operation of market forces. Property then became more or less an absolute and exclusive right and the concept of rights of access in one's property began to disappear. Property was less a matter of access to a benefit. The law was utilized to this end by the passage of the Inclosure Acts[3] in the nineteenth century which appropriated common land to benefit of individuals in a market economy. What was of value in this economy was the exchange value of the land and not its access benefit or its revenue benefit.

This transformation of property was complete by the early twentieth century and comprises the basis of the 1925 property legislation, where the number of legal estates was reduced to two, overreaching and registration were stipulated, and the trust for sale was automatically imposed in specific situations, so that all these changes were designed to effectuate the easy transfer of land from one person to another. Land soon became, not an end, but a means to an end. It was no longer primarily for the benefit of right holders who wanted to fish in its rivers, or to chop wood on its grounds, or to hunt in its forests. Some people might indeed want to do just this. Land was now to have the benefit of intangible economic advantages. Land was to become denatured as land. It was what you could do with land in terms of insurance and securities and capital that was important. In the later twentieth century, it was possible to say, therefore, that land had disintegrated into discrete areas. It was possible to say, as Professor Roger Cotterrell said, that 'property is dead as a result of having been worked to death in indiscriminate legal application'.[4]

Reich's New Property and the Social Trust

In 1964 Professor Charles A. Reich wrote his seminal, and now oft quoted, article on 'The new property',[5] which he described as revenue-type rights on which a person's livelihood and security today depend. These rights are therefore deserving of legal protection. The rights include welfare benefits, state employment, state franchises, state contracts, state subsidies, licences to exercise a profession and so forth. Reich was fundamentally concerned with the distribution of wealth, benefits and advantages from the state which were provided as 'government largesse'.[6] Although Reich did not deal with traditional property law rights his new property theory was wide enough to apply between private individuals where there is a similar power relationship of control and dependency. The important thing to remember is that these rights are predicated, not upon any contractual relationship between the claimant and the government or other private individual, but upon the status that the claimant wishes to assert. This may be the status of a professional who requires a licence to earn a livelihood, or it may be the status of a sick person who wishes to have access to welfare benefits, or it may be the status of an unemployed person who wishes to take back his job. Professor Roger Cotterrell has observed that it is difficult to decide which particular status claims will be protected.[7]

However, it is submitted that the reference to status rights by Reich is only another way of referring to a person's citizenship rights, for it is only in consequence of the wider development of modern citizenship rights that he is enabled to lead a more fulfilling life and to lay a claim to broader economic, social and political rights. Put another way, in those countries that are tyrannical and oppressive it is not meaningful to speak of status because their subjects do not have a developed notion of citizenship rights in the form of which we speak in liberal western democracies. At the same time, the categorization of rights as citizenship rather than as status rights has the merit of allowing us to think not only about what our rights may be in a more focused way, but also about what our liabilities may be. For example, one can talk about the liability or responsibility of a financial institution that has lent money to a borrower who has become bankrupt to hold the social benefit of his property on a social trust for his benefit as long as is practicably possible. D. W. Large has defined the social trust as 'an inherent public right that transcends the technicalities of title'.[8] Wealthy individuals and institutions that hold the social trust are in a position to control the property for the benefit of a claimant. If judges made it their business to look upon this relationship as a social trust they could be developing a concept of citizenship rights and facilitating a more equitable distribution of important welfare resources. Judges should feel able to go along with the idea because there is a clear social benefit that arises from the imposition of a social trust upon a controlling party. Another way of referring to these controllers is to see them as nominee-owners and this is how Professor Kevin Gray sees them when he observes that 'under the regime of "new property" it can be argued that a "social trust" is imposed upon such nominee-owners by the conferment of status related rights of enjoyment vested in deserving beneficiaries'.[9]

According to Professor Alice E. S. Tay the idea of a social trust is not without its difficulties. She well recognizes that it would require immense and fundamental changes in the concept of property and its regulation through law. She states that 'it is a radical political demand for the socialisation of large scale property and social institutions'.[10] The idea of a social trust, however, would be less problematic if it could be seen as being integral and implicit in the idea of citizenship rights worked out in practice through the presentation of a 'Brandeis Brief', which we will discuss later in this chapter. It would form part of a civic responsibility that the strong have in relation to the weak, allowing the weak, who may already suffer from an inequality of bargaining power, to live in a stable, dignified and pluralistic society. The alternative is a rapacious society. It is unnecessary to legislate. It is unnecessary to formally enshrine the notion of a social trust in the law. It is sufficient simply for judges to exercise their discretion in a way that has this effect. The exercise of discretion by the courts can instil procedural and substantive safeguards in favour of the claimant which would be less radical than adopting more formal means, but yet be no less effectual.

It is in this way that the concerns of Professor C. B. Macpherson, that capitalist property rights can only be upheld if governments recognize democratic pressures to give more effective expression to rights of access as an individual right to all society's members, can be met.[11] For a developed democracy whose subjects all enjoy full citizenship rights, property rights must have moral foundations if they are to be integral to the sense of a developed democracy. The moral basis of such property suggests that it must be a property that allows the redistribution of power and affects the relationships of control and dependency in society in a way that guarantees to the individual access to property and participation in the redistribution of those resource assets. What this redistribution of resources is intended to do is to give protection to the individual's basic human rights, such as the right to adequate housing, the right to medical services, and the right to employment protection.

The social trust is only a notional concept in the desire to achieve these ends. The social trust, symbolizing an egalitarian social contract between the controller and the claimant, is however a good notional means of securing basic fundamental rights for citizens in a community. Reich himself was not calling for a radical restructuring of property law. He was not calling for 'new' property rights in his 'new property'. Although he does end his discussion with the statement that 'we must create a new property' this has been criticized by Professor Alice E. S. Tay as a mere 'rhetorical flourish'.[12] Reich's discussion in his article was merely intending to draw attention to the dangers of wide administrative discretions in the distribution of social benefits (which had become the new property) and he was calling for control over the exercise of these discretions; he was not seeking to vest, in recipients of the new property, rights of social benefits or any new proprietary claim on the benefits that they received. His theory was therefore advocating a protection of the claimant of these benefits against unfair or improper official exercise of discretion in the conferring or withholding of such social benefits.

Although Reich was not calling for a restructuring of property entitlements, he did recognize that a discriminatory policy could be put in place so long as it was relevant to a social benefit. This recognizes a redistributive element to the apportioning of property rights in society. Within the ambit of those conferred property rights, the claimant is inviolable. Thus Reich conceives property rights in ways that suggest not entitlements but benefits:

> property draws a circle around the activities of each individual or organisation. Within that circle, the owner has a greater degree of freedom than without. Outside, he must justify his actions and show his authority. Within, he is master, and the state must explain and justify any interference . . . . Thus property performs the function of maintaining independence, dignity and pluralism in society by creating zones in which the majority has to yield to the owner.[13]

It was because of the benefits of such rights that Reich felt able to criticize the decision of the court in *Flemming* v. *Nestor* which had denied old people 'a stable, dignified and independent basis of retirement'[14] by refusing a state pension to the contributor's widow. In a subsequent article, which became the sequel to 'The new property', Reich referred to these rights as basic human rights.[15] Again, it is submitted that the notion of human rights, like the notion of citizenship rights, is far more intuitively appealing, and therefore workable, than the idea of 'The new property' or 'The social trust'.

Human Rights, the Social Trust and Citizenship

Unlike the preoccupation with procedural rights which characterizes much of traditional property law, human rights is also an idea which can be used to advance substantive fairness in decision-making and it can be pegged on to citizenship rights. Thus Steiner and Alston, in their book *Human Rights in Context*, refer to the variety of human rights rhetoric that can be drawn upon:

> The list of internationally recognised human rights is by no

> means immutable. Just as the British sociologist T. H. Marshall characterised the 18th century as a century of civil rights, the 19th as that of political rights and the 20th as that of social rights, so too have some commentators over the past two decades put forward claims for recognition of the new rights, in particular a category known as the 'third generation of solidarity rights'. By analogy with the slogan of the French Revolution these rights have been said to correspond to the theme *Fraternité*, while first generation civil and political rights correspond with *Liberté* and second generation economic and social rights with *Egalité*. Karl Vasak's list of solidarity rights includes 'the right to development, the right to environment, the right to ownership of the common heritage of mankind and the right to communication'.[16]

The attraction of this approach is that there is none of the difficulty about when a claimant's right can be classified as a personal right in property. There are a number of methods that can be adopted to protect rights on this basis. For example, it has been suggested by Professor C. B. Macpherson that the social trust principles that form the bedrock of the social trust doctrine can be assimilated into a new common law where the 'equitable' redistribution of proprietary rights can take place. The law can be made to move full circle and return to its feudal basis of property rights defined in terms of community rights of access and enjoyment for mutual social benefit, rather than as a right to exclusive ownership.[17] Another method that has been proposed is that of statutory regulation which should supplant the common law in this field. Professor Alice Tay has argued that the private common law is not a suitable medium for effecting new developments in the control and regulation of property. She considers that 'the task is to distinguish between the various types of property, for the purpose of framing specific and appropriate legislation and regulation'.[18] The purpose here is to set up a statute-based administrative system which regulates and controls rights of access to social benefits. This certainly has an advantage over the previous method because it seeks to transfer the protection of a claimant for rights of social benefit from a private law system into a public law system, and from an adjudicative system of justice to an administrative one. This view has attracted widespread support from other theorists.

It is submitted, however, that there is a third option that falls somewhat in between and that citizenship is the best means to augment the utilization of this third option. There is now a developing canvass of statutory provisions which seek to protect precisely those rights which can be categorized as rights to social benefit. This is to be seen from the spate of legislation starting from the protection afforded to residential tenants and licensees under the Rent Acts[19] and the Housing Acts,[20] to the protection of residential status for wives who register a class F land charge under Section 1 of the Matrimonial Homes Act 1983,[21] to safeguarding residential security against a spouse's trustee in bankruptcy under Section 336 of the Insolvency Act 1986.[22] These are statutory provisions and yet their ultimate effectiveness depends upon the exercise by a judge of a *common-law* discretion. The question is how this discretion should be exercised. Traditional time-worn principles of equity, being based upon 'good faith' and 'unconscionability', may be inadequate in establishing social benefits for claimants. A discretion that is based upon an appreciation of citizenship rights in the community would have the advantage of incorporating the social trust doctrine because it would be based upon an egalitarian social contract between the parties. It would protect human rights. Yet it would obviate the need for a pervasive and comprehensive statutory regulation to stipulate in detail social benefit property rights. A discretion that is based upon these grounds would be radical enough to enable a court to strike down a controller's decision to refuse or deny social benefit rights because in appropriate cases the courts can apply differentiating provisions, particularly in areas of unequal bargaining positions, provided that there is a clear social gain to society. Eventually there will emerge a unified doctrine in Land Law which will provide for a universal system for safeguarding the right of an access to a social benefit.

Bankruptcy and Domestic Residence Rights

We will now consider the bankruptcy cases in this context. The social benefit that is being considered here is the use of premises for domestic residence. The situation that a claimant faces here arises from a trustee in bankruptcy requesting the court to sell the family home for the benefit of creditors, with the resultant eviction of the family from the home. Bankruptcy case law is a fertile area in which to study the application of citizenship values. There is here a direct conflict between the commercial interests of creditors, who often represent big business, and the security of domestic tenure for ordinary individuals and their families. The court has to mediate between this direct conflict. The most common scenario in the case law is the husband or common-law spouse who cannot pay his debts as they fall due. These may be unsecured business loans or they may be mortgage instalments, including other debts. When he cannot pay, either the creditors or the husband himself applies to the court for a receiving order. The court assesses his assets and liabilities and declares him bankrupt and a trustee in bankruptcy is appointed to administer his estate. A co-owner who becomes bankrupt has his estate defined so as to include also his property to which he is beneficially entitled. Indeed, the bankrupt co-owner's most valuable asset may well be his interest in his own home.

Under Section 306(1) of the Insolvency Act 1986, the bankrupt's entire estate vests in the trustee as soon as the appointment takes place. Under Section 305(2) the trustee comes under a statutory duty to realize the bankrupt's assets. It is his job to get in, realize and distribute the bankrupt's estate. The trustee will have to obtain the best price on sale. To do this he will have to sell the house with vacant possession. If the property is co-owned and held on trust for sale, the non-bankrupt co-owner may be unwilling to agree to the sale. If so, the trustee in bankruptcy will have to apply to the court under Section 30 of the Law of Property Act and the court will have a wide discretion to decide whether to evict the family of the bankrupt co-owner, and if so, under what circumstances. Section 30 is in the following terms:

> If the trustees for sale refuse to sell . . . or any requisite consent cannot be obtained, *any person interested* may apply to the court for a vesting or other order for giving effect to the proposed transaction . . . and the court may make such order as it thinks fit . . . (Emphasis added.)

Since the court has a wide and unfettered discretion under this provision, it is instructive to see how this discretion is exercised. We will examine all the decided cases over the last thirty years since this is roughly the period over which the major social and economic changes in our society have taken place. We will discover that without an adherence to citizenship principles the right to residential security has not generally been upheld by the courts. We will see that the equitable jurisdiction of the court has not come to the aid of families threatened with eviction. Yet the courts could have had a real impact in this area, particularly because the insolvency law provisions in the 1986 legislation are less sympathetic to the bankrupt's family than was envisaged in the original proposals of the Cork Committee in 1982, and the courts through an exercise of a discretion unfettered by statute could have leaned over backwards to protect the interests of the family. The 1986 legislation provides limited rights of residential security for the family. Section 336(3) of the Insolvency Act 1986 requires an application under Section 30 to be made where the bankrupt and his spouse or common-law spouse were both trustees for sale of the matrimonial home. Section 336(2) provides protected statutory rights of occupation under the Matrimonial Homes Act 1983 to a bankrupt's spouse who is not a trustee for sale of the house.[23]

However, the provisions in Section 336 do not apply to co-owners and co-habitees. They only apply to a husband and wife. This was contrary to the recommendation of the Cork Committee. Under Section 337 there is new protection to a bankrupt who assumes responsibility for his children but has no spouse occupying the family home with him,[24] thereby providing statutory rights of occupation that are akin to those of the Matrimonial Homes Act 1983. Finally, there is a reference in Section 336(5) and Section 337(6) to 'exceptional circumstances',[25] but this has not been interpreted objectively by the courts, but only in reference to the existing case law which has assumed that the meaning to be ascribed to the term 'exceptional circumstances' is synonymous with the one-year breathing space in those subsections which would provide a period for the bankrupt and his family to find alternative accommodation.

The first important case on the family right to residential security is *In re Soloman* in 1967.[26] Here the husband and wife were joint legal owners of their matrimonial home which was purchased on the strength of a mortgage. After matrimonial differences between the two, the husband left the wife. In the matrimonial proceedings that followed, the husband was ordered to pay the mortgage interest and all household outgoings and to permit his wife to occupy the house rent free for life. Later, the husband fell ill and was unable to keep up the payments, ran out of business, and was adjudicated bankrupt on his own petition. The trustee applied under Section 30 of the LPA 1925 for an order for sale. Goff J held in the divisional court that the wife's right of occupation under the maintenance order was purely personal against her husband. It did not bind the trustee. The court used the test from *In Re Buchanan-Wollaston's Conveyance* where Sir Wilfred Greene MR had said that the court 'must look into all the circumstances of the case ... and ask itself the question whether or not the person applying for execution of the trust for sale is a person whose voice should be allowed to prevail'.[27] This reference to 'whose voice should be allowed to prevail' is at the heart of the Section 30 jurisdiction. It demonstrates how open-ended is the situation when it arises before the court. The court has a complete discretion to decide as it will and make whatever order that it thinks fit. Yet the cases are, almost without exception, in favour of the trustee in bankruptcy.

In this case Goff J gave four reasons why the voice of the wife should not prevail. Goff J's reasoning well illustrates the competing claims that the courts have to balance in this situation. First, the marriage was effectively ended. Although the marriage was still subsisting, the husband had deserted the wife more than ten years earlier. Second, the purchase of the matrimonial home occurred before the breakup of the marriage and was not contemporaneous with the later purpose of providing a home for the wife. Third, the husband had paid the entire initial deposit on the purchase and the mortgage capital and interest with the wife having made little financial contribution to the house. Fourth, the wife's rights would not prevail as against the creditors' legitimate commercial claims 'because this is not a question between the husband and wife, but between the wife and the trustee in bankruptcy on behalf of the husband's creditors'.[28] The court ordered that the property be sold with vacant possession, the trustees be entitled to one half of the net proceeds, and the sale be postponed for a reasonable time to enable the wife to find other accommodation and put her affairs in order.

In re Turner Goff J considered the case of a bankrupt husband who was living with his wife in the matrimonial home. Both the husband and wife were joint tenants both at law and in equity of their matrimonial home. Under Section 30 of the LPA 1925 the husband's trustee in bankruptcy sought an order for sale. At the hearing, the husband and wife appeared in person although the trustee was represented by counsel. Goff J held that making an order for sale was always a matter of discretion for the court even if the home was the bankrupt's only asset. The decision shows how little use the traditional doctrine of equity is in these cases. Goff J held that:

> In my judgement, the guiding principle in the court's discretion is not whether the Bank or the wife *is being reasonable* but, in all the circumstances of the case, whose voice in equity ought to prevail ...[29] (Emphasis added.)

In this case, the wife had tried to rely on two cases in vain. In *Jones* v. *Challenger*[30] in 1961 it was held that where property is acquired jointly as a matrimonial home neither spouse has a right to demand a sale under Section 30 of the LPA while that purpose still exists. This applied to joint occupants, whether married or unmarried, but the application of the principle depended on the whole of the beneficial interests being vested in the occupants, which it could not be if one of them became bankrupt since the beneficial interest would then be vested in his or her trustee. Goff J held that 'the wife is not entitled to pray in aid the *Jones* v. *Challenger* (1961. 1 Q.B. 176) line of cases and is not entitled to deprive the husband's creditors in the bankruptcy of their share in the matrimonial home'. Once again, the decision reflects, in a short judgment, the conflictual claims to property rights that arise under Section 30. As Goff J said:

> in my judgment, there exists in equity two conflicting claims: on the one hand the wife as part owner of the house asks: why should she as co-owner be turned out merely because her husband, the other co-owner is bankrupt? On the other hand the trustee in bankruptcy says he is not only entitled to realise the husband's interest but is bound by statute to do so.[31]

However, it is respectfully submitted here that the court could exercise its discretion on the basis of an evaluation of the social effect of its decision, in terms of both benefits and burdens. Who does this decision benefit and who does it burden? What is the impact in society of deciding one way as against another? How much leeway can the court give? That this is not the conventional approach of the courts in this area is evidenced by Goff J's reference to his fourth reason *In re Soloman*, and the reiteration of that reason, that the issue was between the wife and the trustee. This was not an issue to do with the matrimonial home. Goff J continued that, furthermore, 'weighing the two conflicting claims, that by the Trustee based on his statutory duty, gives him the stronger claim and requires me to treat his voice as the one which ought to prevail in equity'. This is unsatisfactory. It negates the discretionary basis of the power under Section 30. It is a questionable principle because it suggests that a trustee will always have a better claim against the occupants of a home because the trustee has legal obligations to secure the assets of the estate. It is a short step from this to argue that there is a *prima facie* right to sale in all such cases.

The decision *In re Densham* in 1975 provided further grounds for pessimism. Here again Goff J considered yet another case of a bankrupt husband living with his wife in the matrimonial home, although here the wife's interest in it was less than half. However, the house was always regarded as a joint purchase and was bought using joint savings. The legal title was not vested in joint names, however. The husband was not a person who aroused much sympathy. He had stolen monies totalling £13,000 from his employer to lead a lavish lifestyle. He then took out a second mortgage to pay for some household improvements. The thefts were discovered and the husband was convicted. In a subsequent action by the employer to recover the sums stolen, the husband was declared bankrupt. The trustee applied for sale. The case does not add anything of general legal value to the earlier authorities. However, for the first time in a bankruptcy case, consideration was given to the effect of there being young children of the marriage. Counsel for both the husband and the wife stressed the possible harmful effects of the sale of family property on the children. However, Goff J held that this had only an indirect bearing on the matter. Consideration was given to the wife's nervous illness caused by the troubles, but this was also discounted. The wife had been reckless in spending the stolen money. On the other hand, the creditor was the victim of the bankrupt's theft. The trustee had a statutory duty to secure sale. There was a lack of other available assets. Importantly, there was an absence of any remedial purpose in postponing the sale. Goff J held that 'where, as here there are no other assets and the co-owner is not in a position to make any proposition to the trustee, his voice should normally prevail in equity'.[32]

This is a very strict view of the provisions. It suggests that the bankrupt will only prevail in a limited number of cases where the circumstances are other than normal. The court clearly does not contemplate a rigorous exercise of judicial discretion. Nor does it consider social benefit to be a proper exercise of discretion. Thus Goff J was able to say that the order was for sale postponed for a 'generous six months'. In addition, 'a further factor of no small importance is that the local authority is trying to find alternative accommodation, and, in fact, has made one offer'. While the court may be doing all to prevent the family from suffering any further hardship, such an approach does not demonstrate a concern for preserving residential security.

In re Bailey (A Bankrupt)[33] in 1977 the court faced a situation where the parties had been divorced in 1974 and the husband became bankrupt a year later. The wife contended that the order for sale should be postponed. She had a son who was waiting to complete his full-time education in the summer of 1978. The husband had debts of around £4000. The County Court ordered that the wife should have three months until 1 October 1976 to raise £3000 for the trustee, and if this were possible then the sale would be delayed until 1 May 1977. If it was not achieved, then sale would take place on 1 November 1976. The wife failed to raise the sum of £3000 and appealed against the order of the County Court judge. The Divisional Court of Bankruptcy rejected the appeal and ordered sale within a short period. There was considerable discussion as to how far the interests of the children could be taken into account and both Sir Robert Megarry VC and Walton J thought that their interests were only incidentally to be taken into consideration. The Vice-Chancellor observed that the dispute was to do with the son's education because he had commenced A-level studies and the wife was pressing for a postponement of the sale until the summer of 1978 when he would have completed his studies.

The court was influenced by the decision in *Burke* v. *Burke*[34] in 1974, that the interests of the children are only incidental. The Vice-Chancellor held that the matrimonial property cases were not cases in which matters of commercial obligation arose, as the case of bankruptcy where the claims of the creditors as asserted through the trustee in bankruptcy must be considered. The same attitude of giving primacy to matters of commercial obligation was shown by Walton J. He accepted that the children's welfare was a big factor:

> But when one has cases which are between the trustee in bankruptcy and a former spouse, or, indeed, an existing spouse (because it sometimes works out that way) of the bankrupt then the situation is vastly different ...[35]

However, this surely is a question of discretion – nothing more and nothing less – and the principles upon which such discretion is to be exercised. Different judges, with different policy objectives, will exercise this discretion differently.

Lord Denning, for example, always laid great store on the importance of the family, and its impact on the fabric of society. In *Williams* v. *Williams* in 1976, in a case where the two trustees for sale had been divorced but the plaintiff's ex-wife continued to live in the property with the children of the marriage, he had emphasized the principle that

> when judges are dealing with the matrimonial home, they nowadays have great regard to the fact that the house is bought as a home in which the family is to be brought up. It is not treated as property to be sold, nor as an investment to be realised for cash. The Court, in executing the trust, should regard the primary object as being to provide a home and not a sale. Steps should be taken to preserve it as a home for the remaining partner and children, but giving the outgoing partner such compensation, by way of a charge or being bought out, as is reasonable in the circumstances ...[36]

In re Bailey[37] it was argued that the *dicta* in *Burke* v. *Burke* that family interests were only incidentally to be taken into account should be reconsidered in the light of *Williams* v. *Williams*. The judgment in *Williams* v. *Williams* could have paved the way to the development of a family-based residential security jurisprudence. This would have rejected the strict legal constructionist approach *In re Densham*[38] and would have had important social consequences for our communities.

However, one reason why our courts have traditionally failed to use human rights as a tool to effect beneficial social change is because they do not place their decisions in the appropriate social context. They do not look at all the social facts that surround the case. They concentrate simply on the primary facts between the disputants before them. Courts in this country, for example, could adopt a variant of the 'Brandeis Brief' which was developed by Louis D. Brandeis in 1908 when practising for the Supreme Court. This is a brief that uses legal arguments relying heavily on factual materials to demonstrate that a law is or is not reasonable. Traditional briefs are combinations of legal citations and earlier decisions and they emphasize that courts should follow existing law. Brandeis wanted to emphasize that innovative laws could also be valid. The brief that he developed gave short shrift to legal citations, confining them to merely two pages, and included over a hundred pages of factual information from the United States and European countries to demonstrate that it was not unreasonable to believe, for example, that excessive hours of labour were detrimental to the health of women and their families.[39] Brandeis therefore developed a relationship between societal need and the law through a summary of the relevant facts. As a justice on the Supreme Court, he discovered that not enough lawyers were practising the art of putting together 'Brandeis Briefs' and that their arguments contained too little factual information. His theory of attorney responsibility was then broadened to include a theory of judicial responsibility. If attorneys failed to include the factual data to provide rationality for a proposed course of legal action, then he would have his clerks seek out such social facts as were necessary to include in his opinions before giving judgment.[40]

It is not known what the effects of a failure to honour a commercial obligation to a bank is. It is certainly known, however, that a failure to provide some leeway for a family suffering from the effects of mortgage default is damaging to family life and contributes to homelessness in society. The high rate of possession proceedings in the late 1980s and early 1990s is well known and its deleterious effects on poverty and the economy are public knowledge. Judges should encourage the citation of social information in the courts based on hard facts and statistics and should, moreover, take pains to give judgments that address such concerns. Instead, the court *In re Bailey* did not give consideration to the social effects of its decision. Megarry VC observed that the house was the husband's only real asset, and realizing the husband's interest would be a way of allowing him to pay his entire debts. If, on the other hand, the sale were delayed, then the low statutory interest, 'unhappily still a mere 4%', would prejudice his creditor's claims. The court recognized the difficulties that would be facing the family, but preferred this to a situation where the debts went unpaid. The sale of the home would allow the wife to receive a sum of £6000, which was recognized as not being a very large sum with which to seek another home, and it was recognized that the wife would have difficulties finding a place that was suitable for both herself and her son.[41] The approach of Walton J was even stricter. It simply applied the common law, the maxim *pacta sunt servanda* had to be observed and 'a person must discharge his liabilities before there is any room for being generous. One's debts must be paid, and paid promptly, and, if they cannot be paid promptly, then the trustee in bankruptcy must take over.' Although Walton J acknowledged that the court had a discretion in these matters, he felt that 'there are nothing like the sufficient special factors here for the court to delay a sale'.[42] The reference to 'special factors', it is submitted, indicates the considerable evidential burden that resides on a defendant occupant in these proceedings.

The court's judgment gives further grounds to believe that, even though it has wide discretion to make such order as it thinks fit, it is not approaching the disputants' competing claims on the basis of parity and equity in looking at the hardship appertaining to each side, and that the court does not approach this question on an equalitarian basis. Thus, Walton J considered the arguments in favour of postponing the sale to be less compelling. He likened this to the case of the family living in a house specially adapted to the needs of a handicapped child, which house now had to be sold. On the other hand, he considered the hardship pertaining to the bank to be more severe. If he were to postpone sale, he would have to consider the likelihood of the creditors being paid in full, what they would have to pay by way of interest for any borrowing they may have to incur, and so on. Consequently, he concluded that 'having regard to the present day economic climate, the hardship to them of not being paid immediately would be very considerable indeed'.[43] This unduly disfavours and burdens family interests as against commercial interests. A decision such as this certainly cannot be rationalized on the basis of a return from contract to status: it is contract pure and simple. It does not even consider whether the hardship to the bank is avoidable.

In re Holliday,[44] decided in 1981, we find the only judicial authority giving protection to family residential security. Unlike the other cases, here a sale within a short period was not ordered. The property here was in joint ownership. The husband deserted his wife and their three children and remarried. The wife brought proceedings for a property adjustment order against the husband and the husband then immediately filed a bankruptcy petition and was adjudicated bankrupt. An order for sale of the matrimonial home was subsequently applied for by the trustee in bankruptcy. The wife responded by launching a motion to annul the adjudication. Foster J dismissed the wife's application and made an order for sale. On appeal, the Court of Appeal (Buckley LJ and Sir David Cairns) held that the circumstances of the wife and the children were such as to justify postponing the sale for five years and two months. According to Buckley LJ:

> The wife finds herself saddled with the burden of providing a proper home for the children, which she would not be capable of doing out of her own resources ... that situation is attributable to the former conduct of the debtor in leaving the wife and family and going to make himself a new home for himself with another lady. This seems to me to afford the wife strong and justifiable grounds for saying it would be really unfair to her to enforce the trust for sale. Of course, the creditors are entitled to payment as soon as the debtor is in a position to pay them. They are entitled to payment forthwith; they have an *unassailable right to be paid* out of the assets of the bankrupt but in my view, when one of those assets is an undivided share in land in respect of which the debtor's right to an immediate sale is not an absolute right, that is an asset in the bankruptcy which is liable to be affected by the interest of any other party interested in that land, and if there are reasons which seem to the court to be good reasons for saying that the trust for sale of the land should not be enforced, then that is an asset of the bankruptcy which is not immediately available because it cannot be immediately realised for the benefit of the creditors.[45]

This judgment, however, does not evince an intention to protect family residential security any more than the other cases.

This was a case where, crucially, the creditors were not pushing for repayment. The husband owed debts of £6510 and the sale of the house would have provided him with a sum of £13,250 – ample capital with which to meet the demands of his creditors. On the other hand, the wife was living in a three-bedroomed house with three children aged fifteen, twelve and seven. It was obvious that the debts would be paid in due course! As Sir David Cairns said, whereas it would have been difficult for the family 'to find an alternative home' the sale would be postponed

> because it is highly unlikely that postponement of the payment of the debts would cause any great hardship to any of the creditors; and because none of the creditors thought fit themselves to present a bankruptcy petition and it is quite impossible to know whether any of them would have done so if the debtor had not himself presented such a petition.[46]

The exercise of discretion referring at length to the difficulties of the wife and the children has the appearance of having been undertaken on an equal basis, treating both parties as equal in every way. This however is wholly deceptive. The equalitarian approach to the determination of Section 30 rights has not been adopted by the courts in bankruptcy cases. The dicta of the court are ample proof of this.

In re Lowrie (A Bankrupt)[47] in 1981 the court reverted to the requirements of strict hardship from those asserting a right to residential security by requiring their circumstances to be 'exceptional'. The matrimonial home in this case was in the sole name of the husband who had paid the deposit for it. The remainder was advanced by way of a mortgage of which about half the instalments were paid by the wife. The husband took out the loans to pay off the instalments as they fell due, but he could not repay all of them. His trustee in bankruptcy applied to the County Court for an order for sale, which order was made but suspended for thirty months. The trustee then appealed successfully to the Divisional Court in bankruptcy, which ordered a sale within a short period. This was despite the fact that an immediate sale would have caused great hardship to the family of two young children.

The observations of the Divisional Court (Goulding and Walton JJ) are revealing. Walton J held that:

> One must always look at the whole of the circumstances of the case, and in *exceptional circumstances* there is no doubt that the trustee's voice will not be allowed to prevail in equity and the sale will not be ordered. A brilliant example of just such a situation is to be found *In re Holliday (a bankrupt)* . . . where the petition in bankruptcy had been presented by the husband himself as a tactical move, and quite clearly as a tactical move to avoid a transfer of property order in favour of his wife or ex-wife at a time when no creditors whatsoever were pressing and he was in a position in the course of a year or so, out of a very good income, to discharge whatever debts he had.[48] (Emphasis added.)

After reviewing all the facts in detail, Walton J came to the conclusion that there were no exceptional circumstances which justified a postponement of the order for sale. It may be argued, of course, that the circumstances of a family with two young children *are* exceptional. Indeed, Goulding J could not bring himself to agree precisely with such reasoning. Nevertheless, he agreed that the trustee in bankruptcy's appeal should be allowed. To him, the task at hand was not at all simple, because 'the court ... has to effect a comparison of merits and hardship which *in its nature is very difficult*, because the position of creditors on the one hand and a family on the other *are in themselves hard to compare*'.[49]

This, it is respectfully submitted, is a most revealing observation for it recognizes that in order to protect both sides sufficiently, the court has to examine them in as equal a manner as possible. The fact is that here one is not comparing like with like. An equalitarian approach would view their prospects from their respective positions, of both advantage and disadvantage, before undertaking an evaluative comparison of their respective merits. It is because the comparison is undertaken on an inherently unequal basis that it is possible for Walton J to say with equanimity that:

> It is desirable to step back for a moment and look at the situation which must in these cases inevitably occur, or at any rate must occur so frequently as to be almost inevitable. *The first one is that the whole family are going to be rendered homeless. That is not an exceptional circumstance.* It is a normal circumstance and is the result, the all too obvious result, of a husband having conducted the financial affairs of the family in a way which has led to bankruptcy. The second result almost invariably is that it is going *to be incredibly hard* and incredibly bad luck on the co-owner, the wife who is in most cases *a totally innocent person* who has done nothing to bring about the bankruptcy. Of course, as against that, one has to realise that she has been enjoying over whatever period it may be, the fruits of the debts which the bankrupt has contracted and which debts at the moment are not being paid.

At present, such is the imbalance in the exercise of judicial discretion under Section 30 arising from a strict constructionist approach of the law, that it is possible for Walton J to go on as follows:

> [T]he money which the bankrupt owes to his creditors year by year is steadily diminishing in value as the worth of the property increases, and *the princely rate of interest* laid down under the bankruptcy legislation of 4% was the rate laid down in times when the value of money was stable and bears

> no relation to what is happening today, so the situation undoubtedly is that there will be *totally unlooked-for and unnecessary hardship* on the creditors if they are kept out of their money for *any appreciable length of time*.[50] (Emphases added.)

The worst aspect of such an approach that does not give vent to the rights of citizens on a principle of parity and equity is the tendency of writing off people who cannot pay their debts as they had contracted to do. This may not always be the result of profligacy on their part. It may simply be bad luck. The court's approach may be perfectly consistent with the common-law approach which requires a man to be as good as his bond. Yet, such an approach does nothing for the development of fair discretionary rules and powers under Section 30.

In re Mott[51] in 1987 is noteworthy because it is the second reported case where residence was protected on the grounds that circumstances were exceptional. Here the wife was a seventy-year-old widow living alone in a house 'full of memories' as she had lived there forty years with her late husband. She was in ill health and her condition would have deteriorated had she been moved. The property was owned jointly by herself and her son who had been declared bankrupt. The creditors were the DHSS and the Inland Revenue. An application for sale was made to the Divisional Court by the trustee in bankruptcy. Hoffmann J held that it was difficult to imagine a more extreme case of hardship. He balanced the legal and moral claims of the wife's and the son's creditors and concluded that the creditors must wait until the wife's death before sale of the house. Clearly, therefore, moral claims are not irrelevant.

In re Gorman (A Bankrupt)[52] in 1990 the husband and wife purchased a house with the wife paying one-third of the purchase price, and remainder being raised on the mortgage, and the property being registered in the names of both parties. The wife paid all the mortgage instalments. The husband and wife then divorced. After the husband left, the wife remained in the matrimonial home with their two children. The husband was later declared bankrupt, with his interest in the matrimonial home being his only asset. At the trial, the house was valued at £100,000 with an outstanding mortgage debt of £5000. When the divorce had occurred, the wife's solicitors had negligently failed to apply for a property adjustment order. Therefore, the wife had a potential course of action against her solicitors.

The trial judge, hearing the trustee's application for sale, held in the County Court that, notwithstanding the statement of joint ownership at the land registry, the wife in fact owned the entire beneficial interest because she had paid the deposit and all the mortgage instalments. The trustee's application for sale was therefore redundant. Interestingly, however, the trial judge observed that had he been required to exercise his discretion for sale, he would have granted a postponement of two years to allow the wife to bring a negligence claim against her solicitors. This indicates the exercise of a broad discretion that sympathetically gives consideration to the full circumstances of an occupant's predicament.

On appeal, the Divisional Court (Vinelott and Mervyn Davies JJ) held that the joint tenancy that existed on purchase continued until bankruptcy. On bankruptcy, the tenancy was severed into equal shares. The husband's interest having then vested in the trustee in bankruptcy, the latter owned half the beneficial interest in the house, subject to the equitable accounting for the wife's improvements to the land. Vinelott J held that the trial judge in the County Court had attached too much weight to the existence of the negligence claim. In his view, the trial judge had

> failed to give proper, or indeed any, regard to the financial hardship that will be suffered by the trustee and the creditors, if the sale is deferred for an indefinite period which may exceed two years. The creditors have already been kept out of their money for very many years during a period of high interest rates, and regrettably, inflation, and can look to nothing except the proceeds of sale of the property to pay a dividend on their debts.[53]

In this case, seven years had lapsed since the bankruptcy of the husband, and although the court referred to the 'hardship' to the bank by this delay in the payment of their debts, the court was not without sympathy to the plight of the wife. However, in evaluating the respective hardship of the two parties, it has to be remembered that this was a house to which the husband had made no contribution. It was hardly surprising, therefore, that he had gone off leaving the wife and two children in the house, as Vinelott J observed:

> I am not without sympathy for Mrs Gorman, who faces the prospect that a house, to the purchase of which Mr Gorman in the event made no contribution, will be sold to pay his debts. She has lived there for many years and brought up the children in circumstances of great difficulty.[54]

However, to what extent would the court give effect to these moral claims as against the strict legal claims of the creditors? No doubt, the wife also had legal rights. Why should she be required to give up residential security? In the event, Vinelott J proposed an innovative order. He proposed that the proceedings be stood over subject to appropriate conditions including the payment of interest, to give the wife time to complete her negligence action on the basis that she would use the damages awarded her to buy out the trustee in bankruptcy, for a sum equal to the share of the proceeds that would be taken by the trustee on sale. The court in this case is giving firm protection to the creditors' interest. It is only considering postponing the sale subject to these conditions, with the market rate of interest being payable by the wife. The judgment by Vinelott J is to that extent different from the trial judge, who was minded to give protection to the wife's interest.

In re Citro (A Bankrupt)[55] in 1990 is a much-analysed bankruptcy case because it reviews all the authorities in some detail. Here two brothers, Domenico and Carmine, were adjudicated bankrupt in 1985 following the failure of their joint business, after they owed about £123,000 in tax. Their only assets were their interests in their respective matrimonial homes. Each brother had three children. Domenico was separated from his wife, but she continued to live in the house with the children. Carmine lived, on the other hand, in the matrimonial home with his family, but was awaiting divorce proceedings. The trustee in bankruptcy applied for the sale of the two houses under Section 30. In 1989, Hoffmann J ordered sales of the two houses but postponed enforcement until the youngest child of each brother was sixteen. Hoffmann J took into account that each wife had very little money herself and Domenico's wife was, in any event, ill. If the houses were sold immediately, the proceeds might not have enabled the wives to find proper accommodation for their families. The trustee in bankruptcy, however, appealed the judgment by Hoffmann J.

In the Court of Appeal (Nourse and Bingham LJ and Sir George Waller) the appeals were allowed (with Sir George dissenting) and the sales ordered, subject to a postponement of six months. Nourse LJ reviewed the authorities to date. He referred to *re Bailey* where Walton J had spoken about the existence of 'special factors' as a prerequisite for the exercise of discretion in an occupier's favour, and referred to *re Lowrie* where Walton J had required there to be 'exceptional circumstances' before deciding that the trustee's voice would not be allowed to prevail in equity. He then concluded as follows:

> In my view Walton J, in describing the circumstances in which the trustee's voice will not prevail as 'exceptional', stated a correct test. Alternatively, he might have described

> them as 'special' which to my mind means exactly the same thing.

What, however, was to be the effect of requiring circumstances to be exceptional upon judicial decision-making? Nourse LJ gave his answer thus:

> The broad effect of these authorities can be summarised as follows. Where a spouse who has a beneficial interest in the matrimonial home has become bankrupt under debts which cannot be paid without the realisation of that interest, the voice of the creditors will usually prevail over the other spouse and a sale of the property ordered within a short period. The voice of the other spouse will only prevail in exceptional circumstances. No distinction is to be made between a case where the property is still being enjoyed as the matrimonial home and one where it is not.[56]

Nourse LJ then moved on to examine what the exceptional circumstances may be; however, he did not provide any answer to this question. This failure to provide clear guidelines on the exercise of judicial discretion under Section 30 is disturbing. The statutory provisions do not require rights of occupation to be exceptional before they are deemed to be deserving of legal protection; in any event, eviction from home is surely an exceptional event for most families. Yet Nourse LJ now held:

> What then are exceptional circumstances? As the cases show, it is not uncommon for a wife with young children to be faced with eviction in circumstances where the realisation of her beneficial interest will not produce enough to buy a comparable home in the same neighbourhood, or indeed elsewhere. And, if she has to move elsewhere, there may be problems of schooling and so forth. Such circumstances, while engendering a natural sympathy in all who hear of them, cannot be described as exceptional. They are the melancholy consequences of debt and improvidence with which every civilised society has been familiar.[57]

With respect, however, if this is right one might just as well say that death is the melancholy consequence of improvidence and one which every civilized society has throughout time had to deal with. Surely, such weighty issues cannot be brushed off so lightly if one is setting out to do justice.

The point is that there is wide discretionary power under Section 30 for the courts to deal with these matters and to protect the residential security of families who have fallen on hard times and are being driven into homelessness at the behest of large corporate businesses. Given his premises, Nourse LJ had little difficulty explaining why Hoffmann J's decision in the court below was wrong. He gave three reasons:

> First . . . the personal circumstances of the two wives and their children, although distressing, are not by themselves exceptional. Secondly . . . the judge erred in fashioning his orders by reference to those which might have been made in the family division in a case where bankruptcy had not supervened . . . Thirdly, and perhaps most significantly, he did not ask himself the critical question whether a postponement of payment of their debts would cause hardship to the creditors.[58]

For his part, Bingham LJ was more troubled by the consequences that befell the family enjoying rights of occupation in bankruptcy cases. Although he concurred with the judgment of Nourse LJ, he added:

> I should for my part have inclined to think that a test of exceptional circumstances was, in the absence of statutory guidance, more stringent than was warranted . . . but I have to acknowledge that in enacting Section 336(5) of the *Insolvency Act 1986*, Parliament appears to have expressly approved it.[59]

Bingham LJ thought that the decision of the court below was open to criticism because it did not distinguish *re Holliday* for the following reasons:

> (i) that *In re Holliday*, unlike the present case, there might well have been no bankruptcy at all but for the debtor's action; (ii) that after the moratorium imposed by the court all the creditors could be paid in full with interest . . . (iii) that the sum available to the wife on sale was expected to be much smaller . . . than would be available to either of these wives; (iv) that the children in that case were younger than those in these cases.[60]

Re Holliday was, of course, the case where the petition in bankruptcy had been presented by the husband himself as a tactical move to avoid a transfer of property order in favour of his wife at a time when no creditors were pressing. He was then in a position in the course of a year to discharge whatever debts he had. But the children in that case were aged sixteen, thirteen and eight years.

In the present case, however, Hoffmann J had postponed the sales on the basis that the youngest child of each brother should reach sixteen years of age, which was not to be until 1994 and 1995 respectively, that is, five years' and six years' time. Nevertheless, Bingham LJ comes the closest so far in the Court of Appeal in adopting an approach that is conducive to the protection of citizenship rights by adopting an equalitarian approach that looks to the position of both from the viewpoint of a level playing field. The other judge who has done so, so far, is Hoffmann J in the Divisional Court. This is evident from what Bingham LJ had to say about the approach adopted by Hoffmann J below who had

> treated *re Holliday* as entitling him or obliging him *simply to balance* the interests of the creditors against those of the wife, the creditors' prima facie entitlement to their money being *simply one element in the scales* – and not a particularly weighty one at that. I would willingly adopt this approach if I felt free to do so. It is in my view conducive to *justice in the broadest sense* and it reflects the preference which the law increasingly gives to *personal over property interests*. I do not, however, think it reflects the principle which, as I conclude, clearly emerges from the cases . . . as I have, I think, made clear, I regret this conclusion.[61] (Emphases added.)

The approaches of Bingham LJ and Hoffmann J, in the court below, in this case indicate that the position adopted by Nourse LJ requiring 'exceptional circumstances' is not necessarily right, whether as a question of social fact or as a question of statutory law. Indeed, it is questionable whether the principle *pacta sunt servanda* applies in these circumstances since in most cases it is the wife and the children who suffer and yet they are not the ones who have entered into contract with the principal creditor.

This indeed was the view taken by Sir George Waller in this case, who simply dissented from the majority judgment of Nourse LJ and Bingham LJ. He reviewed the earlier cases and came to the conclusion that *re Holliday* was indeed directly relevant to the issues here. He followed Goff LJ in that case that

> balancing the interests of the creditors and the interest of the wife, burdened, as I say, with the obligation to provide a home for the three children of the marriage, in my view the right attitude for the court to adopt is that the house should not at present juncture be sold.[62]

Sir George Waller, accordingly, agreed with Hoffmann J below that the positions of the wives in this case were 'extremely unenviable' which was not different from 'hardship' or 'very special circumstances'.[63] *In re Citro* is a text-book case for the study of judicial discretion in property cases. Three judges, on the same facts, held three different positions: Nourse LJ that the position of the two wives was not exceptional; Bingham LJ that the wives' position *was* exceptional but that he was bound to hold that it was not; and Sir George Waller that their position was exceptional and that he was bound to hold that it was.

The Court of Appeal decision *In re Citro* and the reconciliation of the bankruptcy cases with each other was analysed by the same court again in *Abbey National plc* v. *Moss*[64] in 1993. Here a mother had been persuaded to transfer her house into the joint names of herself and her daughter on the understanding that she would have a right to live there with the property remaining unsold for the rest of her life. Subsequently, her daughter acquired a loan on the joint mortgage of the house by forging the signature of her mother on all the documentation. She then moved out of the house and defaulted on the repayments. The creditors applied for an order for sale under Section 30.

The Court of Appeal (Peter Gibson and Ralph Gibson LJ) held that the *ratio* of *In re Citro* meant that the secondary purpose (that the property be occupied as a matrimonial home by the daughter) ended when her husband became bankrupt and his beneficial interest in the house vested in his trustee in bankruptcy. This was because the joint occupation of the home was based on the joint ownership of the beneficial interest. However, where the secondary purpose is not based on joint ownership – such as here where the collateral purpose was to provide a home for the mother for the rest of her life – there the purpose may continue even if one of the co-owners disposed of or charged their beneficial interest. In these circumstances, it is for the person who seeks the order for sale to persuade the court that the order can be properly made. However, Hirst LJ dissented from this judgment. He held that the *ratio* of *In re Citro* contained the wider proposition that where a trustee in bankruptcy of one co-owner makes an application for sale under Section 30, there is a presumption that a sale will be ordered unless there are exceptional circumstances.

This principle had been applied to the application by a chargee under a charging order against the equitable interest of one co-owner in the case of *Lloyds Bank plc* v. *Byrne and Byrne*[65] in 1991, and it should be applied also to the 'almost identical position' of a mortgagee of the equitable interest of one co-owner by a majority; therefore, the Court of Appeal in this case refused to make an order for sale. This brings to a total of three the number of reported cases where a sale has been refused. This hardly provides grounds for any optimism that the courts are reaching out to protect the right of occupation of a person to residential security. However, even though the great majority of cases are decided in favour of the party applying for an order for sale, the principles cannot be said to be clearly well established. The conflict between personal and property interests remains and has yet to be satisfactorily settled.

Charging Orders and Domestic Residence Rights

The reference above to the case of *Lloyds Bank plc* v. *Byrne and Byrne* in 1991 requires us at this stage to deal with the related area of charging orders. In this case the Court of Appeal held that the principles that apply to an application by a trustee in bankruptcy were also applicable in the same way to an application by a chargee under a charging order obtained against the equitable interest of one co-owner. Charging orders involve the creditor requesting the court to appropriate the home to provide security for the discharge of a debt, rather than the trustee in bankruptcy requesting the court to sell the family home for the benefit of the creditors. Residential security is as much at stake in relation to charging orders as it is in relation to applications by trustees in bankruptcy. This is because the charge of the property has the effect of conferring an interest in the home on the chargee with the result that it confers a *locus standi* upon the chargee enabling him to apply for a sale of the home under the Law of Property Act 1925.[66]

The charging order is made when an order of the court is given in favour of a judgment creditor. At first a charging order *nisi* will be granted.[67] Once a notice has been served on any trustees of the property and on any other person as the court may direct, the chargee may apply for the order to be made absolute. The order then operates as if it were an equitable charge agreed by the debtor, by writing under his own hand. Unlike bankruptcy, the charging order only entitles the creditor to apply for the sale of the property to which the charge applies. If the charge applies to the matrimonial home, the creditor can only sell the beneficial interest therein. Under Section 3(4) of the Charging Orders Act 1979, however, the creditor obtains an interest in the property that is charged. This can be of great significance. As a person interested, he has *locus standi* to apply under Section 30 of the LPA 1925 for a court order. The court order will direct the trustees to execute the trust for sale. This will result in the entire property being sold free from all the interests of the beneficiaries. The debt can then be satisfied from the debtor's share in the proceeds of sale. The starting point, however, is always the order of court in favour of a judgment creditor granting him a charging order. The decisive question is with what ease or difficulty such an order can be obtained from the court. It is clear that it is not to be granted as of right. Section 1(5) of the Charging Orders Act 1979 is as follows:

> In deciding whether to make a charging order the court shall consider *all the circumstances of the case* and, in particular, any evidence before it as to –
> (a) the personal circumstances of the debtor, and
> (b) whether any other creditor of the debtor would be likely to be unduly prejudiced by the making of the order. (Emphasis added.)

Once again, discretion is very important in deciding whether or not to make a charging order. This discretion operates at two levels. First, there is the discretion under Section 1(5) which includes both the personal circumstances of the debtor and the rights of other interested third parties. Second, there is the discretion under Section 30 of the LPA which structures the shape of the final order.

The first decided case that arose after the passage of the Charging Orders Act 1979 is *National Westminster Bank Ltd* v. *Stockman*[68] in 1981. The property was vested in the joint names of the husband and wife both in law and in equity. A charging order was applied for by the creditor bank over the husband's beneficial interest in the home and was refused by the Master. It was held that an interest under a trust for sale was not an interest that could be properly charged under Section 2 of the Act. Section 2 is in the following terms:

> (i) a charge may be imposed by a charging order only on –
> (a) any interest held by the debtor beneficially –
> (1) in any asset of a kind mentioned in subsection (ii) below, or
> (2) under any trust
> (b) the assets referred to in subsection (i) above are (a) land.

The creditor bank appealed to the High Court whereby the Queen's Bench Division allowed the appeal. Russell J held that:

> In my judgement it was plainly the intention of the legislature that the availability of charging orders should be extended to cover cases in which the interest sought to be charged is beneficial interest in the proceeds of sale of land

> held under a trust for sale . . . There are various safeguards available to the debtor when application is made to make the order absolute and to his wife whose position can be protected in the event of any application by the creditor which would have the effect of defeating the purpose for which the trust was established.[69]

The reference to 'various safeguards' here suggests that the wife has adequate protection through the exercise of judicial discretion under Section 30 of the LPA 1925. It is of course true that before an occupant can be evicted there must be a Section 30 application at the hearing of which the wife will have the right to make representations to the court. However, as we have seen from the cases above, it is quite clear that the courts do not exercise a free discretion, but have bound themselves by self-imposed guidelines that severely restrict the cases in which an occupying wife may succeed in protecting her residential status. A charging order *nisi* was granted by the court in this case.

In *Cedar Holdings Ltd* v. *Green*[70] in 1981 the court exercised the Section 1(5) discretion in a way that favoured the wife in occupation, although this was a case that did not involve charging orders. Both husband and wife were joint tenants at law and in equity in the matrimonial home. A *decree nisi* was granted in divorce proceedings. The husband, with another woman posing as his wife, then executed a legal charge over the freehold property in favour of the plaintiff creditor who sought an order for sale on the grounds that the husband had charged his beneficial interest to the creditor.

This claim was dismissed by the Court of Appeal on two grounds. First, it was held that the property charged was expressed to be 'land' whereas the husband only owned an interest under a trust for sale, which did not bring it within the provisions of Section 63 of the LPA 1925. Secondly, as Goff LJ stated:

> where the vendor has some estate or interest in the land, albeit less than he contracted to give, the court will not order specific performance to the extent of his true estate or interest 'where the alienation of the partial interest of the vendor might prejudice the rights of third parties interested in the estate' (see Fry on specific performance, 6th edn, p. 588, para 1270). Such specific performance would, as it seems to me, prejudice the other co-owner in two ways. First, while the matter remains in contract she has at least a well arguable case for saying that the first defendant has not made a disposition of his share, so that she can claim protection

> under Section 16 of the Matrimonial Property and Proceedings Act 1970 . . . In any case, whether or not the court would ultimately order a sale under Section 30 of the Law of Property Act 1925, such specific performance must be *prejudicial to her position* in proceedings against her under that section.[71] (Emphasis added.)

It is clear from this that the court regards the effect of a Section 30 application to be inevitably detrimental to the interests of the wife, and it is a shame that this reality of the *de facto* state of Section 30 jurisdiction is not grasped more frequently as a discretion that is always heavily constricted by commercial considerations. What the court is doing here is recognizing the fact that once the door is opened to allow a Section 30 application to be made the odds are heavily laid against personal rights of occupation.

In *Thames Guaranty Ltd* v. *Campbell*[72] in 1984, the matrimonial property was purchased by the husband and wife and held jointly both at law and in equity. Before the conveyance took place, the company agreed with the husband alone, without the wife's consent, to grant him a loan which was secured by first charge on the property. After the land was registered in joint names, the creditor increased the sums loaned to the husband on two further occasions. The husband then became bankrupt. The creditor brought proceedings against the husband, claiming to be a secured creditor on his beneficial interest.

At first instance, Mann J held that there was no actual charge granted, but only a specifically enforceable agreement to create a charge. The court would not therefore exercise its discretion and order a partial performance, to the extent of the husband's interest, of that agreement. Following *Cedar Holdings* v. *Green*, he held that if the grant of specific performance would have been prejudicial to the wife in that case, then it would be prejudicial here also. In relation to Section 30, he further held that:

> If an order were made in favour of the company it would prejudice the right of the wife as a joint tenant to the *occupancy of the matrimonial home* in that she would be exposed to proceedings under Section 30 of the Law of Property Act 1925 at the instance of a secured creditor, which would be *very likely to result in an order to sell.*[73] (Emphases added.)

Once again, this is a clear recognition of the fact that the Section 30 discretion does not provide realistic judicial protection for the interests of the wife in occupation.

On appeal, the Court of Appeal upheld the decision of the trial judge, but on different grounds. Slade LJ held in relation to the Section 30 discretion that

> [t]he discretion of the court is a real one . . . Mrs Campbell's occupation cannot be disturbed by the plaintiffs until an application has been made under Section 30. In the submission of counsel for the plaintiff, that would be the appropriate stage to consider which of the competing equities are entitled to prevail, in the light of full evidence as to Mrs Campbell's personal and family position. This would appear to accord with the views of Bingham J as expressed in the *First National Securities Ltd* v. *Hegerty* [1984] 1 All ER 139, especially at 143.[74]

It is, of course, the case that there is no judicial recognition of the weakness of the Section 30 jurisdiction to protect the personal right to occupation in property. Quite the contrary, in fact. Yet Slade LJ does in the next breath acknowledge the weight to be attached to creditors' interests:

> We see much force in the submission that the mere fact that an order for partial performance in cases such as at present would give the chargee *locus standi* to apply for sale under Section 30 should not, by itself *necessarily deprive an innocent chargee of the remedy of part performance*.[75]

Yet Slade LJ upheld the decision at first instance against the creditors on the grounds that 'they have largely been the architects of their own misfortune, in failing to require Mr Campbell to perfect the charge',[76] since the creditors had known of the wife's interest and had continued to deal with the husband alone and were now seeking to intervene detrimentally against the wife under Section 30 proceedings.

First National Securities v. *Hegerty*[77] (referred to above) in 1984 concerned the exercise of discretion under Section 1(5) of the Charging Orders Act. Both the husband and wife were joint tenants at law, but their beneficial interests were not clear. The husband had borrowed money, but used another woman to represent his wife to charge the matrimonial home as security for the loan. A charging order *nisi* was obtained over the husband's beneficial interest by the creditors. Divorce proceedings were then commenced by the wife against the husband. The husband agreed to transfer his interest to the wife. The wife was successful in having the charging order discharged whereupon the creditors appealed.

Bingham J in the Queen's Bench Division held that the charging order should be reinstated and made absolute. He held that a judgment creditor has a *prima facie* right to a charging order. The wife could only displace the charging order if she showed good reason why the court should refuse to exercise its discretion under Section 1(5) of the Act. The judgment by Bingham J leaves no doubt that the burden falls squarely on the wife enjoying rights of occupation to demonstrate why a charging order should not be used, for he had found 'nothing in the circumstances of the case which begins to displace the lender's *prima facie* entitlement'.[78] His Lordship made short shrift of the prejudice caused to the wife:

> So I turn to the main submission of counsel for the wife. This is that the appeal should be dismissed as the making of a Charging Order absolute would be *unfairly prejudicial to the wife* . . . Now the making of a (Charging) Order would necessarily restrict to some extent the benefit she could obtain (i.e. under a property adjustment order). For that reason no order should be made and the options opened to the Family Division judge (when considering a property adjustment order) should not be in any way circumscribed. I accept that these are matters to be considered among 'all the circumstances of the case' but I do not think that they weigh very heavily against the *legitimate claims of the lenders* . . . Moreover, I accept that the wife's possession of the house cannot be disturbed until there has been an application under Section 30 of the 1925 Act and a full hearing at which the wife's personal and family position can be investigated. That is the stage for finally determining which of the competing voices is entitled in equity to prevail.[79] (Emphases added.)

This strict view of judicial discretion by Bingham J was not only upheld but commended on appeal.

The Court of Appeal held that the issue was simply whether or not the judge below had erred in law by exercising his discretion wrongly. The Court of Appeal (Stephenson and O'Connor LJJ and Sir Denys Buckley) approved the approach adopted by the High Court. Stephenson LJ (with O'Connor LJ concurring) added only the following contribution:

> (1) the court should not use its powers under part two of the 1973 Matrimonial Causes Act (on ancillary relief following divorce) to override the claims of a creditor seeking security for a debt by a charging order;

> (2) it should discharge or vary a charging order so as to prefer a wife's claim to such a creditor's,
> (3) it can, and often should, postpone the enforcement of a charging order until the hearing of an application under Section 30 . . .[80]

By all accounts, the prospects for a wife who in equity not only jointly owns the premises that are charged, but who is not consulted either, are so grim as to amount to a denial of justice. The court had usurped a discretionary power to enforce sale as a matter of course in a way that could not have been the policy of the Act. It is seen to be giving free sway to monied might rather than protecting the interests of vulnerable parties who most need the protection of the law in society.

The case of *Harman* v. *Glencross*[81] (1984) was decided at first instance before Stephenson LJ had occasion to give his judgment in the Court of Appeal in *Hegerty*. The Appeal Court had clear opportunities, therefore, of witnessing an alternative approach to the exercise of judicial discretion. Here the husband, who owned his home jointly with his wife, borrowed monies from his business partner. Divorce proceedings were then commenced by the wife with notification being given to the creditor. The proceeds of sale were likely to be divided up equally between the husband and wife. The creditor then obtained a charging order over the husband's beneficial interest. The wife applied for the charging order to be postponed pending the outcome of her ancillary proceedings for financial relief and property adjustment.

The charging order was held by the registrar to be subject to those proceedings. In those proceedings the husband's entire beneficial interest was ordered to be transferred by the registrar to the wife. The registrar's decision was followed by Ewbank J in the Family Division who agreed that the charging order should be subject to the ancillary proceedings. Indeed, he regarded the reasons for this to be 'overwhelming' and he distinguished the *Hegerty* decision in the High Court, which went on to be upheld on appeal in the Court of Appeal, as follows:

> [I]t was because of the charge of the home which the creditor thought that he had that the money was lent. This, in my judgement, was a compelling consideration *which does not exist in the present case*. . . . if it is right in accordance with Section 1(5) of the 1979 Act, *that all the circumstances of the case are to be taken into account* before a charging order is made, I cannot help feeling that leaving a decision until an application under Section 30 of the 1925 Act is made is *failing to do justice to the*

> *wife. After all, under Section 30, the only real question that the court is concerned with is*, how long is the wife to continue to have possession and not whether there should be a sale at all.[82] (Emphases added.)

In this case, we see a radical departure in the exercise of judicial discretion. Whereas other judges had started from the premise that a creditor has a *prima facie* right to judgment, Ewbank J negates that premise by calling for a freer discretion to be exercised under Section 1(5) to forestall the effects of a Section 30 decision, in order to do justice for the wife, simply because he knows that 'all the circumstances of the case' have not normally been considered when the Section 30 discretion has been exercised.

This tells us two things. First, it tells us that a judge who is truly concerned about the social ills of residential insecurity can do something about it by bringing his discretion to bear on his decision-making in a way that protects the person's continued right of occupation in the home. This is done in this case by giving priority to the property adjustment order over the charging order so that the creditor loses his proprietary security interest as well as, more dramatically, any hope of recovering his debt, because the husband's only asset has been transferred to his wife. Second, and of far more general importance, the exercise of a radical discretion in this case is telling about how much the Section 30 discretion has become a dead letter today. The judge here was forced to adopt an ingenious device only so that he could exercise a freer discretion which he knew that he could no longer do under Section 30 since that section had been severely restricted in its application by previous case law.

On appeal by the creditor to the Court of Appeal, that decision by Ewbank J was upheld.[83] Balcombe LJ also gave three further guidelines. First, if a judgment creditor applies for a charging order to be made absolute before the wife begins divorce proceedings, the court should make the order absolute and Section 30 can adequately protect the wife's right of occupation. Second, if the charging order *nisi* is made after the wife's divorce petition then the court should consider whether it would be proper in the circumstances to make the order absolute before ancillary relief proceedings. Third, the Family Division should usually consider the application by the judgment creditor so that one court is in a position to consider all the circumstances of the case and the court should bear in mind that 'a judgment creditor is justified in expecting that a charging order will be made in his favour'.[84] In the words of Balcombe LJ:

> The normal course should then be to *postpone the sale of the house* for such a period as may be requisite to protect the right

> of occupation, a *mesher* type of order . . . If the judgment creditor asks . . . for a *mesher* type of order, then it seems to me that it would require exceptional circumstances before the court should make an order for the outright transfer of the husband's share in the house to the wife thereby leaving nothing on which the creditor's Charging Order can bite, even in the future.[85] (Emphasis added.)

For his part, Fox LJ supported Balcombe LJ's third guideline and observed:

> I would not myself, if exercising the (Section 1(5)) discretion on such facts as the present, normally have thought it proper simply to refuse a charging order . . . I would myself have taken the view on such facts as the present that the charging order should not be discharged, *but that its enforcement should be deferred* during such a period that might reasonably be necessary for the protection of the wife and children.[86] (Emphasis added.)

The importance of this case cannot be overlooked, for the courts have been able to produce the device of a compromise as a juridical concept to mediate between the rights of creditors on the one hand and the rights of occupying residents on the other.

In *Austin-Fell* v. *Austin-Fell*[87] in 1990 the husband and wife bought their property as joint owners at law with a 100 per cent mortgage. The husband then borrowed money from a bank for business purposes. Later, when the husband and wife separated the bank was granted a charging order over the husband's interest. Divorce proceedings were then commenced and the wife applied for financial relief and the discharge of the charging order. Both these issues were heard together by the registrar. He ordered a transfer of the husband's beneficial interest to the wife whereupon the bank appealed.

In the Family Division, Waite J allowed the appeal by the creditor bank following the decision of the Court of Appeal in *Harman* v. *Glencross*. He held that if, after the charging order was paid off, the equity in the house was insufficient to make provision for the wife with accommodation, then the court should strike a fair balance between the creditor and the wife, and not decide that one claim should have predominance by excluding the other. Waite J followed the third guideline by Balcombe LJ in *Harman* v. *Glencross*. He allowed a charging order over the husband's beneficial interest with enforcement postponed for ten years. This would result in the youngest child of the family reaching the age of eighteen years. Once again, this decision is indicative of a compromise by the courts to try and protect the position of both the creditor and the resident wife and her family in the best way possible.

Conclusion

To conclude this chapter, we can say that the Section 30 discretion of the court is not being freely and openly exercised with regard to all the circumstances of the case. The court has not availed itself of the opportunity provided by Section 30 of adapting discretionary decision-making to a society with a changed legal culture that emphasizes personal rights over property interests. Nor has it given sufficient consideration to a changing social climate where family life and social stability is increasingly under threat and is yet seen to be a public value upon which the well-being of our society ultimately depends. To this extent, it needs now to develop a new strategy, and a new emphasis on a concept of citizenship rights, that recognizes both rights and liabilities between the various interests in society on the basis of an egalitarian social contract, that will not only maintain, but enhance the consensus in society.

The record of the courts so far indicates that the exercise of a free and open discretion under Section 30 has been hamstrung by a disproportionate concern for commercial as against social interests in society. Such an approach is not only morally but also legally indefensible. Section 30 in terms conferred a wide and unfettered discretion upon the court. It was not in terms intended to cater for the needs of commercial creditors. Yet this is precisely the mechanism that Section 30 has now become and a manner in which it has been adapted by powerful interest groups to be marshalled against the vulnerable and weaker sections of society. Small wonder, then, that there has been a steadfast failure and even a refusal to develop guidelines – such as, for example, on the meaning of 'exceptional circumstances' to which an occupying wife and her family may become subject. It needs now to be considered how the Section 30 discretion can actually be used to prevent the turmoil and desperation caused by an impending prospect of homelessness that may befall a family, who may very probably have been encouraged by government policy to enter and expand upon business activities.

It is submitted that unless the Section 30 jurisdiction is now developed upon an equalitarian basis, as in terms it was clearly intended, with regards to personal rights which all citizens in the social community can expect, those enjoying residential security will only have an ephemeral recourse to redress in the courts. That cannot be conducive to justice. In the final analysis, the courts need to use the language of 'justice' more than even the language of 'rights'. In cases other than those of bankruptcy, such as those calling for the exercise of discretion under Section 1(5) of the Charging Orders Act, we can be somewhat emboldened by our arguments thus far by the fact that the courts have sometimes given rather more recognition to the right of residential security when exercising its Section 30 jurisdiction here, than in the bankruptcy cases considered above.

For example, although the evidence is indirect, we see that in such cases as *Stockman*, *Campbell* and *Hegerty*, it has been emphasized by the courts that Section 30 allows the court to give a fair weight to the status of continuing residence, with the result that the court has allowed a charging order in the meantime. By contrast, in such cases as *Cedar* and *Harman*, the courts have treated Section 30 as militating against a claim to residential protection, and therefore have declined to make a charging order, with the result that this has protected residents and prevented a later court from interfering with that protection. Undoubtedly, the case of *Austin-Fell* stipulates a compromise position that would work to the benefit of both sides. Through the grant of a moratorium until the youngest child attains majority at the age of eighteen, the court is exercising a protectionist jurisdiction and avoiding having to expose the family to the risk of a Section 30 sale application.

However, there is no reason why such a protectionist jurisdiction cannot be developed under Section 30 as well. There is nothing that inhibits the use of Section 30 in this way. Indeed, if one looks at such cases as *In re Holliday* and *In re Citro* in the High Court one finds that in the first case the Court of Appeal postponed the sale for five years and two months and in the second case, Hoffmann J effectively postponed the sale for six years, to enable the children in both cases to reach the age of sixteen years. It is not immediately apparent why such protection cannot extend to a time when the children are aged eighteen when the age of majority is reached. However, the major difference in the exercise of discretion between the Section 30 bankruptcy sale applications and the Section 1(5) charging order applications is that in the latter case the courts have not developed a doctrine of 'exceptional circumstances' which must be met by the occupants if they are to defeat a creditor's claims against them. However, why is there such a difference? Does it serve any useful purpose? If not, is its imposition in one case but not another an indication of arbitrariness?

An argument that this divergence in approaches can be explained on the basis that the bankruptcy cases involve a trustee in bankruptcy's statutory duty to sell as well as the execution of performance of the co-ownership trust under Section 30, does not rationally indicate why these arguments did not weigh heavily with the Court of Appeal and the High Court in *In re Holliday* and *In re Citro* respectively. The truth is that the test of 'exceptional circumstances' is a harsh and unwarranted test and it only heaps hardship upon those who are already subject to hardship. The courts must develop a framework of approach that is not only rational, coherent, and practically useful, but is fundamentally just.

Notes and References

1 Macpherson, Charles B. (1975) Capitalism and the changing concept of property. *Feudalism, Capitalism and Beyond* (ed. Kamenka and Neale), p. 110. Canberra.
2 Cotterrell, Roger (1986) The law of property and legal theory. *Legal Theory and Common Law* (ed. W. Twining), p. 92. London.
3 These Acts were finally consolidated in the Inclosure Act 1845.
4 Cotterrell, Roger, *op. cit.*, p. 87.
5 Reich, Charles A. (1964) The new property. *Yale Law Journal* (73), p. 733.
6 *Ibid.*, p. 779.
7 Cotterrell, Roger, *op. cit.*, pp. 86–7.
8 Large, David W. (1973) This land is whose land? Changing concepts of land as property. *Wisconsin Law Review*, pp. 1039, 1074.
9 Gray, Kevin (1987) *Elements of Land Law*, pp. 14–15. London.
10 Tay, A. E. S. (1978) Law, the citizen, and the state. *Law and Society* (ed. E. Kamenka, R. Brown and A. E. S. Tay), p. 14. London.
11 *Supra*, note 1.
12 Tay, A. E. S., *op. cit.*, p. 14.
13 Reich, Charles A., *supra*, note 5, p. 771.
14 (1960) 363 US 603, which decision was cited by Reich at p. 775.
15 Reich, Charles A. (1964–65) Individual rights and social welfare: the emerging legal issues. *Yale Law Journal* (74), pp. 1245, 1257.
16 Steiner, Henry J. and Alston, Philip (1996) *International Human Rights in Context*, pp. 1110–11. Oxford.
17 See Macpherson, *op. cit.*, p. 110.
18 Tay, A. E. S., *op. cit.*, p. 15.
19 The 1977 Act provides protection in the form of rent control and security of tenure for tenants who are 'regulated' and a considerable number of such tenancies remain in existence, despite the fact that such Rent Act protection only applies to tenancies created before 1989.
20 The Housing Act 1988 has replaced the Rent Act in the private rental sector and much reduced the protection that is now afforded to 'assured' tenants only. It may be noted here that the protection afforded to long leases of houses under the Leasehold Reform Act 1967 (ss. 1–4) has recently been extended to long leases of flats under the leasehold Reform, Housing and Urban Development Act 1993 (see part 1).
21 This confers on a spouse who is not on the legal title, statutory rights of occupation in the matrimonial home, which include the right not to be evicted or excluded from the matrimonial home and, if not in occupation, the right with the leave of

the court to enter into and occupy the matrimonial home. These rights constitute a charge on the interest of the other spouse. When they are protected by registration as a class F land charge, they are enforceable against a purchaser from the other spouse: see *Wroth* v. *Tyler* [1974] Ch. 30, pp. 43–6.

22 Under Section 336(2) new protection is afforded to the bankrupt's spouse who is not a trustee for sale but who has statutory rights of occupation under the Matrimonial Homes Act 1983. A charge by a spouse on an estate of the other spouse continues to subsist notwithstanding the bankruptcy, an application for an order under Section 1 has to be made to the court in relation to the bankruptcy, and any application by the trustee of the bankrupt's estate for an order under Section 30 of the LPA 1925 has to be made to the court having jurisdiction in relation to the bankruptcy.

23 *Loc. cit.*

24 This section applies where 'any persons under the age of eighteen with whom that person had at some time occupied that dwelling house had their home with that person at the time when the bankruptcy petition was presented and at the commencement of the bankruptcy'.

25 Both sections are in identical terms and they read as follows: 'where such an application (i.e. an application under section 30 of the LPA) is made after the end of the period of one year beginning with the first vesting under chapter IV of this Part of the bankrupt's estate in a trustee, the court shall assume, unless the circumstances of the case are exceptional, that the interests of the bankrupt's creditors outweigh all other considerations.'

26 *Re Soloman (A Bankrupt)* [1967] Ch. 573.

27 [1939] Ch. 738, p. 747.

28 See Goff J, *supra*, note 26, pp. 588–9.

29 *In re Turner (A Bankrupt)* [1974] 1 WLR 1556, p. 1558.

30 [1961] 1 QB 176.

31 Goff J, *op. cit.*, p. 1559.

32 *In re Densham (A Bankrupt)*, *Ex parte* trustee of the property of the bankrupt versus the bankrupt [1975] 1 WLR 1519, p. 1531.

33 (No. 25 of 1975) [1977] 1 WLR 278.

34 [1974] 1 WLR 1063.

35 Walton J, *supra*, note 33, p. 283.

36 [1976] Ch. 278, pp. 285f.

37 (No. 25 of 1975) [1977] 1 WLR 278.

38 [1975] 1 WLR 1519.

39 The 'Brandeis Brief' was first used in *Muller* v. *Oregon*, 208 US, p. 412.

40 See Mason, Alpheus T. (1946) *Brandeis*, pp. 245–53. New York.

41 See *In re Bailey*, *op. cit.*, p. 281.

42 *Ibid.*, pp. 283–4.

43 *Loc. cit.* In fact, Walton J went so far as to say that 'this may be yet another case where the sins of the father have to be visited on the children, but that is the way in which the world is constructed, and one must be just before one is generous'.

44 [1981] Ch. 405.

45 *Ibid.*, p. 424.

46 *Ibid.*, p. 425.

47 [1981] 3 All ER 353.

48 *Ibid.*, p. 355.
49 *Ibid.*, p. 358.
50 *Ibid.*, pp. 355–6.
51 [1987] *Current Law*, p. 29.
52 [1990] 1 WLR 616.
53 *Ibid.*, p. 629D (per Vinelott J).
54 *Ibid.*, p. 629F.
55 [1991] Ch. 142.
56 *Ibid.*, p. 159.
57 *Loc. cit.*
58 *Ibid.*, p. 159B–D.
59 *Ibid.*, p. 160E.
60 *Ibid.*, p. 161B–C.
61 *Ibid.*, p. 161D–E.
62 *Ibid.*, p. 162H.
63 *Ibid.*, p. 163D.
64 (1993) 26 HLR 249.
65 (1991) 23 HLR 472.
66 Whereupon the court will exercise its well-known discretion under Section 30.
67 See RSC Order 50, R. 1(2).
68 [1981] 1 WLR 67.
69 *Ibid.*, p. 69C.
70 [1981] Ch. 129.
71 *Ibid.*, p. 147.
72 [1984] 1 All ER 144.
73 *Ibid.*, p. 151a.
74 [1985] QB 210 p. 239A–C.
75 *Ibid.*, p. 599.
76 *Ibid.*, p. 600.
77 [1984] 1 All ER 139.
78 *Ibid.*, p. 143.
79 *Ibid.*, pp. 855–6.
80 *Ibid.*, p. 868B.
81 [1984] 2 All ER 577.
82 *Ibid.*, p. 583.
83 [1986] 1 All ER 545.
84 *Ibid.*, p. 559 (quoting Sir Denys Buckley in *Hegerty* [1984] 3 All ER 641, p. 646).
85 *Ibid.*, p. 563.
86 *Ibid.*, p. 564.
87 [1990] 2 All ER 455.

4

Landlords and Tenants

Modern bourgeois property is the final and most complete expression of the system of producing and appropriating products, that is based on class antagonism, on the exploitation of the many by the few – *Karl Marx*

In this chapter, we consider the application of the egalitarian social contract to a species of property relations, namely, the relations between landlords and tenants. We consider also the period, particularly during the first half of the last decade, when the principle of egalitarianism was rejected in preference to a judicially espoused policy of market competition in property relations. We consider next how this was finally rejected in favour of a perspective of egalitarianism that regarded both landlords and tenants as having equally legitimate rights in the renting market. This abandonment of market competition by the courts in favour of the egalitarian social contract does not mean that the courts are imposing a social obligation on landlords to provide individuals with adequate rentable property. It simply implies a tacit recognition that society has a moral obligation to ensure that everyone has access to adequate rented accommodation without being subject to excessive burdens. The obligations here apply to individuals and institutions of all types which play a role in discharging societal services. Thus, these obligations can be enforced through a range of laws and social policies stretching from the Rent Acts to all kinds of social insurance legislation which has the sole purpose of protecting the interests of vulnerable and underserved communities in society.

At the heart of this egalitarian social contract are three components. The first component is the recognition that all sections of the community have legitimate individual rights and interests. These rights are not feudal rights akin to lord and serf or master and servant. They are rights pertaining to the individual in a modern community. They are the rights to belong, to enter contractual relations on an equal basis, to participate in the life of the community, and to lead a fulfilling life. They are rights to communal citizenship. The second component is the realization that those having equal legitimate rights are not necessarily equally situated in society. They are participants, but they are participants in unequal power. They cannot all freely enter into their particular individual contracts. The third component is the belief in the role of the law to achieve a fair resolution of the competing interests between those unequal participants. The law must enforce a 'social contract' that is egalitarian in its nature in order to achieve equitable relationships between all concerned. This is a conception that springs from a debate about whether government and the law should be used as institutions to play a regulatory and egalitarian role, and about the extent to which the economic market should be the organizing model for human relations.

The economic market treats property as a commodity, being dependent upon one's financial strength, whether to buy or to sell. The ideology of market competition began developing in the early 1970s and expanded rapidly in the 1980s and 1990s. It is based upon a strategy of the reduction or elimination of government regulation including common-law remedies in order to greatly increase the power of the players in the market to negotiate through contract. This view can be defended on the basis that, although there may be certain core human and social necessities, such as a need for adequate housing, most people, when they take a property or arrange its financing, do so on the basis of discretionary consumption choices. When people exercise these choices they have their own culturally influenced expectations, but that does not make it necessary to rent a property from one landlord when one could quite easily go to another who can offer different terms.

In support of this view it could also be argued that if those with property could treat it as a commodity with the power to lease it out, then it is illogical to deny consumers and third-party financiers whatever economic leverage they could bring to bear through bargaining and market competition. It could further be argued that regulation, whether by the government or the courts, would not provide a solution because regulatory programmes are notoriously subject to 'capture' by powerful and well-organized regulated interests, who may be landlords or consumer bodies. The ethical imperative is therefore that private decision-making and responsibility should be made paramount by the law and individuals should bear the costs of their individual consumption decisions. It could be argued, therefore, that market mechanisms are more compatible than any other system with society's true ethical, moral and political commitments over the distribution of services and resources in a community. Provided that the individuals understand the alternatives, they should be able to purchase, for themselves, according to their income, what they want.

The egalitarian response to market competition that we shall see in the cases below, however, implicitly rejects these arguments. According to the model of egalitarian social contract, people's current consumption choices and patterns are often made under economic and social pressures and influences, and these cannot be a valid basis of social policy. An individual may rent one property among a myriad others, but such a choice is at least as likely to reflect a painful compromise in the face of economic necessity and limited social options. The egalitarians may also reject the argument that regulation 'captures' markets when one remembers that markets, when operating without regulation, often fail, particularly in relation to the aged, the poor and the most vulnerable. If the individual is sovereign, then market competition in residential rented accommodation is highly unlikely to promote consumer sovereignty. This is because without greater information there is consumer ignorance and dependence and difficulty, in comparing services and prices and terms upon which rented accommodation is made available in the market. Finally, the market competition model is very weak on the issue of equality. A society that is deeply committed to the market as the mechanism for allocating scarce residential accommodation is unlikely to be generous in subsidizing or carefully implementing outreach proposals that target the needs of those who are most vulnerable and most underserved in the residential housing market.

Courts hearing landlord and tenant disputes over the last thirty years have intentionally or unintentionally spoken to all the issues canvassed above. They have both allowed the market to function undisturbed and intervened in the market to curtail its excesses where necessary. They have looked to the parties' legitimate interests. They have proceeded to impose effectively a social contract on all the parties through the medium of the law putting them on a level playing field. We will first consider the statutory framework which bears upon the landlord and tenant relationship and then consider all the decided cases since 1960 in this field.

A person seeking to rent a property has to be careful about the terms upon which such a property is taken. In addition such a person has to be careful about the distinction between a licence and a lease. A licence is less secure because it is determinable upon reasonable notice. A lease of a dwelling house may have the protection of the Rent Acts[1] that will put its grantee into the position of a secure tenant. Since 1988, the Housing Act[2] (see section 1) also now provides assured tenancies under which a landlord has to serve notice and has to gain a court order before he can evict a tenant. However, the Rent Acts are notable for safeguarding residential premises as 'protected tenancies' and as 'statutory tenancies' once the protected tenancy has expired. If a landlord wants to evict he must do so for one of the causes that are listed in Section 98(1) of the Rent Act 1977:

> Subject to this Part of the Act, a court shall not make an order for possession of a dwelling-house which is for the time-being let on a protected tenancy or subject to a statutory tenancy unless the court considers it reasonable to make such an order and either –
> (a) the court is satisfied that *suitable alternative accommodation* is available for the tenant or will be available for him when the order in question takes effect, or
> (b) the *circumstances are as specified* in any of the cases in Part 1 of Schedule 15 to this Act. (Emphases added.)

It is clear from this that if the courts are concerned to protect residential security they should be more willing to make a finding of a tenancy than a licence, for this alone attracts the application of the principles above. A person could not be evicted unless he had suitable alternative arrangements or the Part 1 conditions of the Act are satisfied. As we shall see from the cases below, it is not the case that the courts would necessarily, on past evidence, make a finding of a tenancy in existence. We will see from the cases that landlords are not only in a superior bargaining position, so that they can draft a letting agreement in terms that are characteristic of a licence and declare that the parties intend to create a licence, but they can also avail themselves more readily of the benefits of litigation. Such are the consequences of letting the market function at its whim. What has been most interesting, however, is the attitude of the courts. If the wording of the agreement itself stipulates that the agreement is a licence with a ready power to evict in the landlord, what should the attitude of the courts be? How rigorous is their scrutiny of the terms of the agreement? How often do they look beyond the terms of the agreement to the actual circumstances of the parties before making their decision? To these questions we must now turn. This chapter is divided up into four sections: labels and the nature and quality of the occupancy; non-exclusive possession tenancies; separate agreements with shared occupiers; and local authority occupancies.

Labels, and the Nature and Quality of the Occupancy

Let us first consider some cases chronologically. We will see that the labels and the expressed intentions of the parties are not always synonymous with the nature and quality of the occupancy that is being enjoyed. We will see that the courts have in this situation to make difficult choices in order to elicit the intention of the parties.

In *Barnes* v. *Barrett*[3] the husband and wife had exclusive use of three rooms and a kitchen in part of a house that belonged to a leaseholder. The husband and wife cleaned the part of the house occupied by the leaseholder, cooked for him and paid all the outgoings. They did not pay any rent. When the leaseholder died he surrendered his interest to the freeholder who claimed possession of the house. The County Court held that both the husband and wife were tenants because the services that they rendered to the leaseholder amounted to rent. The Court of Appeal held that husband and wife merely enjoyed a personal privilege of occupation. Sachs LJ drew the distinction between occupational licences and tenancies:

> In this case, as always, it is necessary to give weight to the fact that exclusive possession has been given to the defendants. That however is a factor which is no longer conclusive and indeed *appears nowadays to have diminishing weight*. Weight also has to be given to the words of potential technical import used by the parties. But again these are not conclusive either when written or spoken. In the end it is *the substance of the transaction to which the court must have regard* and when deciding its intended effect it applies to that substance, the law and not the label of either parties.[4] (Emphases added.)

Sachs LJ found that the substance of the transaction lacked the normal incidence of a tenancy since there was no fixed amount of rent and no fixed term and the husband and wife were providing only personal services to the personal taste of the leaseholder. This, therefore, could not be a tenancy. The reference to the 'substance' also indicates that the landlord cannot grant a tenancy and describe it as a licence in order to avoid the effects of the Rent Acts since the courts will have the power to protect the occupier in his Rent Act rights.

In *Buchmann* v. *May*[5] the husband was a tenant who, with his wife, took several successive tenancies of a furnished house for two years. After his work permit expired, the husband had to leave the country. The wife returned to live in the house under a new contract for two months. She claimed she did not read its terms. One of the terms stated that the agreement was 'solely for the purpose of the tenants' holiday'. When the term ended, the landlord claimed repossession of the premises and brought proceedings in the County Court on the grounds that the letting was essentially a holiday letting which excluded it from the Rent Acts by Section 2(1)(b.b.b.)[6] of the Rent Act 1968. The judge held that the court was not 'tied down to the terms of the agreement, but had to look at the reality of the situation',[7] and this was not a holiday letting, despite the clear wording of the agreement. The court is here exercising a discretion which enables it effectively to confer or to deny residential security to a party before it. The court can state that although the written agreement is perfectly clear, its reading of the circumstances outside the agreement leads it to believe that something quite different was intended to what is expressly specified. In the Court of Appeal, however, Sir John Pennycuick VC rejected this approach. He held that the judge had misdirected himself. The judge could not decide the question by reference to oral evidence at large without looking to the written agreement. His Lordship held:

> Where the parties to an instrument had expressed their purpose in entering into a transaction in the instrument, that expression of purpose was at least *prima facie* evidence of their common intention. Clause 6 unequivocally and clearly stated the purpose of the letting.[8]

His Lordship held that the purpose of the arrangement clearly constituted a holiday letting because this is what was specified. However, a decision that is based on what is 'at least *prima facie* evidence' can have the effect of fettering the exercise of a wider discretion that looks not only to the document which expresses the terms of the agreement, but also to the circumstances outside the document which surround the agreement to let. If a landlord with a superior bargaining power can stipulate the terms of the agreement in a document, then the fettering of discretion of the court in this manner can have quite serious effects for what can be defined to be the rights of the tenant. Yet this decision was followed by others subsequently.

In *Horford Investments* v. *Lambert* a landlord let two houses in multiple occupation which were sublet. The head tenant claimed to be a protected tenant. The court simply held that 'the courts have proceeded upon the basis that the *terms of the tenancy are the primary consideration*'.[9] (Emphasis added.) Here residential security was not in issue because the tenant was not in occupation. However, the implications of what the court held would have been serious if the tenant had been in occupation.

In *Marchant* v. *Charters*[10] the Court of Appeal adopted a different approach. A bedsitting room was occupied on the terms that the landlord cleaned the rooms daily and provided clean linen each week. The Court of Appeal held that the occupier was a licensee and not a tenant. The occupier had sought to register a fair rent with the Rent Officer, and the landlord retaliated by commencing repossession proceedings in the County Court. The occupier was evicted and appealed. Although the Court of Appeal held that the occupier was a mere lodger and did not enjoy exclusive possession it gave a broad approach to the interpretation of a letting agreement which was useful to the rights of residential security. In the words of Lord Denning MR:

> What is the test to see whether the occupier of one room in a house is a tenant or a licensee? It does not depend on whether he or she had exclusive possession or not. It does not depend on whether the room is furnished or not. It does not depend on whether the occupation is permanent or temporary. It does not depend on the label which the parties put on it. All these are factors which may influence the decision but none of them is conclusive. *All the circumstances have to be worked out.* Eventually the answer *depends on the nature and quality of the occupancy*. Was it intended that the occupier should have a stake in the room or did he have only permission for himself personally to occupy the room, whether under a contract or not? In which case he is a licensee.[11] (Emphases added.)

It could, of course, be argued that this is not necessarily correct because the nature and quality of the occupancy ultimately depend upon the true construction of the agreement and whether that confers on the occupier exclusive possession. However, Lord Denning here is saying that it is not just the document but all the circumstances which have to be worked out to determine this question. This use of wider discretion indicates that the power to apply or disapply the Rent Acts remains firmly with the court and is not dependent upon the ability of the landlord to define its nature. The landlord is only allowed to evict an occupier if that eviction is consistent with the overall nature of the interest granted. This must make it difficult for landlords to contract out of Rent Act protective legislation.

However, in *Somma* v. *Hazelhurst*[12] the primacy of the document creating the arrangement was re-established by the court. This was to have unwelcome results for quite a number of years. Here a young unmarried couple occupied a double bedsitting room for which they paid a weekly rent. The landlord did not provide services or attendance and the couple were not lodgers but tenants enjoying exclusive possession. The Court of Appeal, however, did not ask itself whether the couple were lodgers or tenants and did not draw the correct conclusion from the fact that the couple enjoyed exclusive possession. The Court of Appeal fell into the mistake of focusing upon the fact that the couple entered into separate agreements with the landlord who reserved power to determine each agreement separately. The landlord also insisted that the room should not in form be let to the couple separately or to both together, but that each should sign an agreement to share the room in common with such other persons as the landlord might from time to time nominate. This was a sham provision. There was never any intention to introduce upon either one of the unmarried couple, who were living together, an obligation to live with someone else. The fact was that the room was let and taken as residential accommodation with exclusive possession by both the couple together. When the couple applied to the County Court for declaration of whether the agreement was for a tenancy or a licence, the County Court found there to be a tenancy, whereupon the landlord appealed. The Court of Appeal held that the separate agreements signed by the couple constituted a grant to the couple jointly of exclusive possession at a rent for a term for the purposes for which the room was taken and the agreement therefore created a tenancy. This was the parties' intention and that intention would prevail. Cumming-Bruce LJ referred to the argument that,

> in a 'Rent Act' situation, any permission to occupy residential premises exclusively must be a tenancy and not a licence, unless it comes into the category of hotels, hostels, family arrangements or service occupancy or a similar undefined special category. We can see no reason why an ordinary landlord not in any of these special categories should be able to grant a licence to occupy an ordinary house. If that is what both he and the licensee intend and if they can frame any agreement in such a way as to demonstrate that it is not really an agreement for a lease masquerading as a licence, we can see no reason in law or justice why they should be prevented from achieving that object.[13]

The court is here returning to a pre-*Marchant* position where a literal approach was adopted. Under this, the terms of the agreement alone determine the existence of a tenancy or a licence. The literal approach allows the court even to contemplate the possibility of a licence being drafted in such a way as to grant exclusive possession of residential property. To come to this view, however, the court has to examine the entire document and not only its particular aspects. However, it is the document that must have primacy:

> So some of these obligations are more consistent with a

> licence than a lease, and some lead to a contrary inference. The balance comes down in favour of a licence because the document cannot be construed as a lease *without substantial re-writing*. (Emphasis added.)

Yet the results of adopting a literal approach are not always fair, and can even sometimes lead to injustice. What if the landlord had extracted unfavourable terms from the occupier purely so as to be able to draft a document that created a licence? The court had no satisfactory answer for this and, in fact, adverted to the possibility of precisely this situation coming about:

> L. has a house. She grants to T. and to W. the right to use one room, but expressly reserves the right to use that room in common with them. On no construction of such a contract can T. and W. claim that they have been granted exclusive occupation of the room.[14]

However, it is simply not realistic in this case to suggest that the couple who were living together as a common-law husband and wife were expecting to be made to share a room with whosoever person the owner may specify. It would appear that the court is allowing here a landlord to stipulate false and artificial terms which will negate or neutralize a tenancy. Yet this is not how the Rent Acts were meant to be applied. By virtue of those Acts, the courts were meant to protect residential security wherever they could. It should have been recognized at the outset that what the landlord was doing in this case was not an option that could realistically have been contemplated in the domain of landlord and tenant law.

In *Aldrington Garages Ltd* v. *Fielder*,[15] the occupier took a flat with two rooms, a kitchen and bathroom. The agreement was called a licence agreement. The occupier only had the right to use the premises in common with another licensee. The landlord had initially shared with another woman who had now left. When the term expired the occupier argued that he was a statutory tenant. The County Court decided in his favour and held that he had signed a tenancy agreement originally, which now made him a statutory tenant. The Court of Appeal, however, found him to be a mere licensee. The court looked at the agreement but interpreted it in the light of the surrounding circumstances. Geoffrey Lane LJ held that:

> It seems to me that if the parties succeed in producing an agreement which, in all the circumstances of the case, is in fact a licence and not a tenancy, they should not be prevented from that course by the courts bending over backwards to

> ensure that landlords do not manage to avoid the provisions of the Rent Acts ... *There is no reason, if it is possible and properly done why agreements should not be entered into which do not fall within the Rent Acts* ...[16] (Emphasis added.)

This is a total infringement of the principle of parity and equality that lies at the heart of citizenship rights because it completely ignores the weak bargaining power of the potential occupier. Whereas the reference in the latter part of this quotation that what is truly a licence should be treated as a licence is welcome, it sits uneasily with the suggestion that the skilful (or even devious) landlord can devise a method to escape the application of the Rent Acts. Even if this were so, this is not something that the courts ought to be encouraging. Given that they are in this case, the recognition that the circumstances outside the agreement can be vital has rather less impact for those interested in promoting residential security as an important public value than it would otherwise have done. The judgment of Roskill LJ was, however, a little less upbeat than that of Geoffrey Lane LJ:

> No doubt the agreements entered into in this *case can be said to be a device* to avoid the operation of the Rent Acts, *but that does not mean that this, or any court, must refuse to give effect to them* if, properly construed against the factual background against which they were entered into, they have the effect for which the property owner contends.[17] (Emphases added.)

In *O'Malley* v. *Seymour*[18] the occupiers of a flat claimed that, although their written agreement defined the letting as a licence, there had been a prior oral agreement which had defined it as a tenancy. They argued that the landlord's attempts now to gain repossession of his flat in the County Court could be defeated by the fact that the written agreement was not consistent with the initial oral agreement which formed the true intentions of the parties. The County Court accepted that there was a prior oral agreement, the terms of which had not been incorporated into the later written agreement. The written agreement, however, contained a clause to the effect that there was no exclusive possession granted. It said that 'the owner grants to the licensee the rights to use the premises in common with others who have been or shall be granted the like right'. The County Court judge thought that this was nothing more than a sham because at the trial the landlord

> was honest enough to admit that he never contemplated for a moment foisting any other persons on the defendant. He knew that the defendant wanted exclusive possession for his

> own purposes . . . both parties here intended that the defendant should occupy the flat for the payment of a periodic sum; the plaintiff intended that to be so and that the defendant would not be disturbed in his occupation of the premises.[19]

The landlord appealed this decision in the Court of Appeal where it was held that the judge had been correct in his conclusions. Stephenson LJ held that,

> Of course (the court) must look at the agreement, but the question whether it discerns there the true relationship between the parties has, in my judgement, already been decided for us by the learned County Court judge. *There was in my opinion clear evidence on which he could have found that this agreement was a sham.* I would go further and say on the evidence before him . . . I should have reached the same conclusion as he did, that it was a sham.[20] (Emphasis added.)

The Court of Appeal has here protected residential status by suggesting that, no matter what the written agreement states, if the document is misleading, then it is not relevant for the purposes of defining the parties' respective rights and interests. The courts are therefore allowing themselves a degree of discretion, to avoid having to take the formal agreement into account, if to do so is conducive to justice in the application of the Rent Acts. The courts will decide for themselves whether the landlord is granting a bundle of rights to the occupier which has the effect of conferring upon him a tenancy. They are doing this fundamentally because of the legal and social interest in protecting residential security, because after all, the occupier has voluntarily signed and accepted the terms of an agreement which he knows to confer upon him only a licence. The way that Stephenson LJ puts it is thus:

> The questions which arise are, it seems to me: first, what on its true construction is the nature of the written agreement on which the plaintiff relied and relies in his claim for possession, against the background of the evidence? Secondly, *does the evidence prove and entitle the judge* to hold that the document, on its proper construction, *does not truly represent or reproduce the real transaction between the parties?*[21] (Emphases added.)

It has to be remembered, however, that this was a case where the owner had conceded that prior to signing the documents or even seeing them, there had been a 'firm verbal agreement' upon which the transaction had been based. The question, therefore, is: would the court exercise its discretion in the same way if there had not been evidence of another 'real transaction between the parties'? It seems that the construction of the document still remains overwhelmingly a matter for the court.

In *Demuren* v. *Seal Estates Ltd*,[22] two postgraduate students were looking for shared accommodation in London. A landlord's agent showed them a flat and discussed the terms for its letting. The students handed over post-dated monthly rent cheques for the entire term. They were given 'licence agreements' to sign. The students did not query the agreements and were not told about the meaning of the terms or the significance of the documents. They sought a declaration that they had the status of protected tenants under Section 105 of the Rent Act 1968 under which a County Court has jurisdiction 'to determine any question ... as to whether a tenancy is a protected tenancy or whether any person is a statutory tenant of a dwelling house'. The judge held that 'in my judgment there was a mutual, concurrent intention of all the parties that the applicants should together have and enjoy exclusive occupation of the whole of the flat' so that they were protected tenants as they claimed. On appeal, the Court of Appeal refused to set this judgment aside. Megaw LJ said,

> In my opinion, there was ample evidence to justify the learned judge in reaching the conclusion that there was such an oral agreement which had been made between the parties before the so called licence came to be signed.[23]

The same conclusion was reached by Roskill LJ who observed:

> I am quite unable to see that the curious and rather ill drawn document that these young men had to sign afterwards in a way necessitates reaching a different conclusion of fact from that which the learned judge reached ... That document simply does not begin to reflect the true transaction between the parties.[24]

Like *O'Malley*, the court has first found there to be in existence an oral contract and then held that to take priority over the formal written contract. However, unlike *O'Malley*, there was in this case no evidence by the landlord of the existence of a prior oral agreement. The law report does not disclose much evidence of a real oral contract. Yet the appeal court has backed the finding of the trial judge. The court is clearly looking to the protective legislation of the Rent Acts to construe contracts in a way that safeguards residential security. An analysis of both the *O'Malley* and the *Demuren* cases at the time suggested that

> what is clear from both of these cases is that the courts will admit evidence of all the dealings between the parties up to the signing of the agreement, *and even of the parties' subjective understanding of the nature of the transaction*, if that establishes that the written agreement does not represent the true agreement and/or the true nature of the agreement.[25] (Emphasis added.)

It is submitted that this is clearly the application of an egalitarian social contract to the principles of landlord and tenant law because it imposes upon the landlord a responsibility by the finding of a purpose, which may be explicit or implicit, behind the agreement. The purpose is often that of providing residential security and of providing protected tenancy security. If the courts were concerned to leave the determination of landlord/tenant relations to the operation of market forces during some of these earlier cases, they would have reached a different result. According to the market, the parties had freely negotiated and voluntarily entered into the agreement that was signed under their hands.

In *Guppy's (Bridport) Ltd* v. *Brookling*[26] the court continued with its protectionist approach based upon an imposed social contract. Here a property company purchased a boarding house and served a notice to quit on all the occupiers in it. Two elderly men had lived in the boarding house for a number of years. They had come to rely upon the services that were provided to all occupiers, which included a janitor who looked after keys, the mail, laundry and did the repairs. The two elderly men refused to leave notwithstanding the service upon them of notices to quit. The company applied to the court for repossession and the two men counter-claimed alleging unlawful eviction. The County Court decided in favour of the two men and awarded them exemplary damages. On appeal, the Court of Appeal held that the trial judge was right in finding a tenancy on the basis of both the written document and the circumstantial evidence:

> The learned judge started with the documentation; I think he was right to do so. It is all very well to talk about slipshod labelling, and of course it is quite right to look at *the reality of the occupation* and not at the labels which the parties put upon it. *Those labels are not conclusive or decisive*, but it seems to me that it all depends on the circumstances of the case as to what weight should be given to those labels, and I think I have read enough of the documents in this case to show that all

> parties, right up to the moment when the claim to possession was made, were treating these occupants as tenants.[27] (Emphases added.)

It is clear from this that the words of the agreement are no longer decisive for they do not on their own determine the nature of the agreement. The court here speaks disparagingly about 'slipshod labelling' and 'the labels which the parties put upon it' in a way that suggests that the courts would rather reserve to themselves the right to determine what the nature of the creature is before them, rather than leave it up to individual persons to decide this for themselves by free-market bargaining. This decision is important in demonstrating a rejection for an initial preference for the signed agreement with the circumstantial evidence being used as an aid to the interpretation of that written agreement. The courts are clearly here moving towards a moral theory of property rights, as against a purely legal one that is determined by technical rules of rights and procedures. As Stephenson LJ continued,

> It is, and I think it should be, very difficult for persons who describe themselves, or treat themselves, as landlords and the occupants of their premises as tenants, *to turn around and say that that was all quite wrong* ... The reality of the situation may be so strong that the court would be driven to reach that position. I do not think it was strong enough in this case.[28] (Emphasis added.)

The imposition of the egalitarian social contract here takes place through the court's insistence that the occupant should not be subjected to inconsistent or unfair conduct by the landlord. The court is insisting upon rules of behaviour that have not only a procedural but a substantive content. Thus the landlord cannot attempt an eviction of the occupant on the grounds that it is a licence that is conferred on the occupant if the courts feel that the occupancy can be protected by being described as a tenancy.

This protectionist approach was, however, rejected in *Sturolson and Company* v. *Weniz*[29] where two contracts were signed for a flat by the first and second defendant occupants. The contracts expressly stated that there would be no exclusive possession of the flat granted. Each licensee would share the flat with the owner and another licensee. The landlord then served a notice to quit and sought repossession. In the County Court the occupants won on the grounds that they had a Rent Act protected tenancy. In the Court of Appeal, a very strict view was taken of the document that all the parties to the agreement had signed. In the words of Eveleigh LJ,

> It is now well established that there is no objection to the owner of the premises granting a licence which will not attract the protection of the Rent Acts as opposed to a lease, but of course he must do so by making an agreement that truly does grant a licence as opposed to a lease.

The statement that it is now established that 'there is no objection to the owner of the premises granting a licence which will not attract the protection of the *Rent Acts*' is certainly debatable and is at variance with the approach of individual judges in other cases. It is certainly an approach that begins with a particular moral stance and then applies the legal rules in the light of that moral stance. It is, however, objectionable because it rejects the protectionist and social contract approach and pays scant regard to the inequality of class in the market place which prevents the market from functioning equitably, with parity and, therefore, to the benefit of all members of society. Despite the landlord having suggested that the occupation would in fact be exclusive, the Court of Appeal rejected the argument by the occupants that the clause dealing with non-exclusivity was a 'sham' and curiously found there to be a licence:

> In view of the answers given by the defendant himself, it seems to me clear that the landlord's agent was indicating to them his expectation of the way in which the landlords would enforce their rights under the agreement; in other words that there would be a benevolent approach to the matter by the landlords. This seems to me to be the only possible way to treat the statement that he expected them to have (occupation) up to the time when the flats would be put in order (since they were being re-decorated). This is quite inconsistent with assuring them that they would have a tenancy, with the security that that implies, but what is more important is that it indicates that the defendant himself knew that this document was governing their legal relationship, what he would not have wanted to know was how the landlord was going to operate it.[30]

Again, this approach is quite contrary to that of previous judges in other cases. The suggestion that the 'defendant himself knew that this document was governing their legal relationship' does not sit convincingly with the view that the defendant 'would not have wanted to know . . . how the landlord was going to operate it' given that the defendant had already sought, and had been given, assurances that 'there would be a benevolent approach to the matter by the landlords'. One could argue that this is not something that landlords are prone to doing, if only because they know, at the very least, the importance of agreeing clear legal terms. This is evident from the way in which the court discussed the relevance of the expressed intention in this case:

> I see no evidence to show that this document was treated as a sham by the landlords . . . the natural conclusion in a case like this would be that the landlord was trying to *achieve an agreement which would in reality defeat the Rent Acts*. That is what the agent said he was doing; that is what the defendant knew he was doing, and it was to such a document that the defendant put his signature. In those circumstances, there has to be very clear evidence that the agreement was something else. Then one asks oneself, if it was a sham what was it that the defendant was seeking to obtain? Who was the defendant intending to deceive? The only purpose in the defendant signing a document with which he did not agree would be to obtain the flat; but he knew that the landlord would not obtain the flat if the circumstances were such that the Rent Acts would apply. Consequently, *he must have known that the legal rights between the parties should be those that resulted from the agreement which was signed*.[31] (Emphases added.)

This is a classic statement of the market orientated approach. It does not look at the circumstances surrounding the agreement. It does not look at the reality of the occupation. It does not seek to ensure fair play and equity between the parties to the agreement. It looks to the document, and to the document alone. It does so, knowing full well that the document can be manipulated to the advantage of the stronger party to the agreement. It ignores human rights as a value. It gives primacy to property rights as against more personal rights of human security. It explicitly rejects the importance of the social protection given to residential security by the Rent Acts, as is recognized by its earlier statement that 'there is no objection to . . . granting a licence which would not attract . . . the Rent Acts'. The approach here is objectionable. This is a case where there had been a direct representation to the defendants that the clause of non-exclusive occupation would not be enforced against them. Therefore, they had acquired *de facto* exclusive possession for the creation of a lease. The approach here is moreover quite incompatible with the approach in cases of prior oral agreements, of sham written terms, and the wide use of surrounding external circumstances that have been deemed to be relevant for the determination of a lease. Yet this was a textbook case for the courts to apply the principle that a party to a transaction must not act inconsistently with the representation that has previously been made.

The decisive turning point in the developing jurisprudence of the lease/licence debate came with the decision of the House of Lords in *Street* v. *Mountford*[32] where a wife, together with her husband, took two furnished rooms in a self-contained flat in a house. She signed an agreement which was called a licence and which concluded as follows: 'I understand and accept that a licence in the above form does not and is not intended to give me a tenancy protected under the Rent Acts.' She did not seek to have these terms clarified by her landlord and the landlord did not offer to clarify them for her. Both occupiers enjoyed exclusive rights of occupation from the beginning of the occupancy and friends of theirs came to see them without the landlord's prior consent. However, when the wife applied for a fair rent registration the landlord sought a declaration from the County Court that her occupancy was a licence and not a tenancy, in order to acquire repossession of the premises. The Recorder found the wife and her husband to have a tenancy of a lease which could not be terminated without a proper notice to quit. He held:

> The agreement document has all the hallmarks of a tenancy agreement. The Mountfords (i.e. the wife and her husband) behaved as tenants. The use of the word 'licence' gives it a false label and it is no less false by the persistence of labelling (the word licence is used nine times).[33]

The Recorder had looked at the overall nature of the occupation in the light of the decision in *Guppy*[34] and *Aldrington*[35] and other cases which followed this line of argument. However, the landlord appealed and the judgment of the Recorder was reversed by the Court of Appeal. The Appeal Court disagreed with the Recorder both on the facts and on the law. On the facts, the Appeal Court could not agree that the written agreement had, in the words of Slade LJ, 'all the hallmarks of a tenancy agreement'. On the law, it held that the express statement of intention in the declaration could not be displaced by the defendant unless it could be shown that it was a deliberate sham or that it was inaccurate as not representing the true substance of the real transaction that was agreed between the parties. A statement made in this way would normally be clear evidence of the parties' intention that the creation of a tenancy was not intended. As Slade LJ said,

> the recent decision of the court in *Somma* v. *Hazelhurst* . . . makes it quite clear . . . that it is legally possible for an agreement to be made between two parties, *even where the*

> *relationship between them is solely of a commercial nature*, under which one of them is to enjoy, and does enjoy, the exclusive occupation of *even a whole house* but is still to have the rights of only a licensee, as opposed to a tenant.[36] (Emphases added.)

This is the strict legal constructionist view once again, giving primacy to the express declarations in the document signed by both parties, rather than to a consideration of the nature of the transaction entered into by the parties. The court is not examining the status of the parties itself but leaving it to be determined by their express declarations in a contractual document, without enquiring into the basis of those declarations. However, even more remarkably, whatever diffidence there may have been in the higher courts before in endorsing a market orientated approach that made it possible for landlords to expressly contract out of their Rent Act obligations, Slade LJ left no doubt that this could be a credible judicial policy on which to base the exercise of their discretion in this field. Referring still to the case of *Somma*, he continued,

> On the authority of that decision I think it must be accepted that it is possible in law for the owner of a building . . . to grant a person the right of exclusive occupation of the top floor without creating a tenancy if he ensure that there is manifested the clear intention of both parties that the rights granted are to be merely those of a personal right of occupation and not those of a tenant.[37]

It would appear from this that a landlord could insert an intention clause in the agreement solely for the purpose of labelling a *de facto* tenancy into a *de jure* licence. If this was right, it made nonsense of the distinction between a lease and a licence. It is not surprising, therefore, that the approach of the Court of Appeal was rejected by the House of Lords. The House of Lords exercised its discretion in a way that recognized that the legal distinction between leases and licences was developed, amended, and maintained in favour of applying the Rent Acts for the purpose of providing residential security, and to this extent, the effect of the agreement was what was critical, and not the intentions that the parties had expressed in the agreement.

It was, therefore, not difficult for Lord Templeman in the House of Lords to disagree with Slade LJ in the following terms:

> Slade LJ reached the conclusion that 'the agreement bears all the hallmarks of a licence rather than a tenancy save for the one important feature of exclusive occupation'. But in relation to the hallmark of exclusive occupation of residential

> accommodation there were the hallmarks of weekly payments for a periodical term. *Unless these hallmarks are decisive*, it really becomes impossible to distinguish a contractual tenancy from a contractual licence save by reference to the professed intention of the parties or by the *judge awarding marks for drafting*.[38] (Emphases added.)

Lord Templeman laid a two-stage test that would determine the existence of a lease or a licence. The first stage is to enquire as to whether the occupier has taken accommodation at a rent for a term. If so, this will give rise to the question whether the occupier is a tenant or a lodger. The second stage is to enquire whether or not the occupier has exclusive possession of premises. If so, then the occupier is a tenant. If not, the occupier is simply a licensee. The degree of exclusive possession can be relevant to the determination of these questions. If the landlord reserves to himself the right to provide attendance or services which give him unrestricted access to the premises then there is no exclusive possession and the occupier is a licensee. On the other hand, if the landlord just expressly reserves to himself limited rights to repair and maintain the premises then this would not take it out of the category of a tenancy. Clearly, the proper approach is to look at the effect of the terms and it would be the court that would determine these effects. It would be the court that would decide both the question of exclusive possession and the question of the intention of the parties to the agreement. These matters would no longer be left up to individuals in the market to determine arbitrarily. Thus, Lord Templeman dealt with the determination of exclusive possession as follows:

> [I]n my opinion, in order to ascertain the nature and quality of the occupancy and to see whether the occupier has or has not a stake in the room or only permission for himself personally to occupy, the court must decide *whether upon its true construction* the agreement confers on the occupier exclusive possession. If exclusive possession at a rent for a term does not constitute a tenancy then the distinction between a contractual tenancy and a contractual licence of land become wholly unidentifiable.[39] (Emphases added.)

On the intention of the parties to the agreement, Lord Templeman had this to say:

> [T]he[40] only intention which is relevant is the intention demonstrated by the agreement to grant exclusive possession for a term at a rent. Sometimes it may be difficult to discover whether, on the true construction of an agreement, exclusive

> possession is conferred. Sometimes it may appear from the surrounding circumstances that there was no intention to create legal relationships. Sometimes it may appear from the surrounding circumstances that the right to exclusive possession is preferable to a legal relationship other than a tenancy . . . But where, as in the present case, the only circumstances are that residential accommodation is offered and accepted with exclusive possession for a term at a rent, the result is a tenancy.

Thus did the court reclaim for itself the power and the jurisdiction to determine whether a landlord had succeeded in contracting out of his Rent Act obligations under an agreement to let out his premises, and the court's exercise of this discretion would no longer be undertaken without proper regard to the social importance of protecting residential security. Landlords will not be allowed to treat property willy-nilly as a commodity for profiteering. As Lord Templeman famously said,

> If the agreement satisfied all the requirements of a tenancy, the agreement produced a tenancy and the parties cannot alter the effect of the agreement by insisting that they only created a licence. The manufacture of a five-pronged implement for digging results in a fork even if the manufacturer, unfamiliar with the English language, insists that he intended to make and has made a spade.[41]

One cannot resist stating here that, whatever the court's intentions in the past, the effect of its exercise of discretions certainly in past cases disclosed a class empathy for landlords in the private sector. For example, one leading authority in property law has recognized that 'there was a growing idea among judges that the parties to an agreement should be free to order their affairs so as to produce a licence' and that this was 'of course extremely good news to landlords who could afford to employ skilled draughtsmen', but that after the House of Lords decision in *Street*, 'some of the straightforwardness of the old law' has been restored with the result that this has 'done many flat dwellers a good turn in the process'.[42]

Street v. *Mountford*, at its various levels – from the Recorder, to the Court of Appeal, to the House of Lords – provides us with a model instance of the different policy choices that individual judges make on a range of legal and social issues which dramatically affect the way in which rights in a community come to be characterized. In one case, and on identical facts, we witness an approach that ranges from a judicial protection of citizenship rights, to a denial of those rights by favouring market economics, and then to its structured recognition through an imposition of an egalitarian based social contract. In addition, the ultimate result in this case differs markedly from the ultimate result in *Somma* v. *Hazelhurst* of which Lord Templeman, in the House of Lords, strongly disapproved. His Lordship said that the agreements in that case constituted the grant to the occupiers of exclusive possession at a rent for a term of premises which clearly created a tenancy. His Lordship accepted that the Rent Acts should not be allowed to alter the construction of an agreement, but nevertheless, the court should be astute to detect and frustrate sham devices and artificial transactions, whose sole object was to evade the Rent Acts. Similarly, His Lordship had little difficulty in disagreeing with the decisions in *Aldrington*[43] and *Sturolson*.[44] However, interestingly, even though His Lordship stated that the Rent Acts should not be used to construe the agreement between the parties, nevertheless, his definition of sham devices, which would open the door to the application of the Rent Acts, was made considerably wider than it had hitherto been.

The established definition of a sham appears in Lord Diplock's judgment in *Snook* v. *London and West Riding Investments Ltd*[45] where shams were defined as 'the acts done or documents executed by the parties to the sham which are intended by them to give third parties or the courts the appearance of creating between the parties legal rights and obligations different to the actual legal rights and obligations (if any) which the parties intend to create'. Lord Templeman, however, replaced the word 'sham' with the word 'pretence' and, in the context of contractual rights, this had far-reaching implications. As Steven Bright commented on this later:

> the Appeal Court in *Somma* had agreed with the judge's finding that the parties knew what they were signing, viz, that the documents represented the true agreement between them and so were not within the *Snook* definition of sham. To see the documents nevertheless as being a sham means that the arrangement is entering into a later stage of the process . . . From the rest of his speech it seems that Lord Templeman was seeking to develop a flexible doctrine, free from the constraints of the *Snook* definition of sham, that would apply wherever an agreement has been artificially structured so as to be tantamount to contracting out of the Rent Acts.[46]

If this is so, then what it does indicate is a shift towards the court consciously eliminating the parties' express contractual terms in favour of upholding the real conditions of the arrangement as the reality of the situation. Once the court has decided to extend its ability to intervene to check pretentious devices, it has effectively diminished the right of landlords to use inventive clauses in order to contract out of their basic obligations to their tenants.

Street v. *Mountford* did not leave all future problems in the law of landlord and tenant unresolved. The House of Lords judgment decided that the nature of the occupation could not be determined by a simple declaration that the parties to the agreement do not intend to create a licence. What they did not decide is what the nature of the occupation would be if the agreement specifically declared that the parties did not intend to enjoy exclusive possession of the premises. Technically speaking, if this were to happen then the arrangement would fall outside the *Street* definition of a tenancy and a landlord would be able to avoid the effects of a protected tenancy. Further, if separate agreements were signed for sharing occupiers then the basis for finding a non-exclusive possession would be even more compelling. However, can such non-exclusive possession clauses be deemed valid or could they be just another pretence designed to avoid the application of the Rent Acts? Let us first consider non-exclusive possession tenancies, which were previously embraced by the courts. Then we will consider separate agreements for sharing occupiers.

Non-Exclusive possession Tenancies

In *Markou* v. *Da Silvaesa* and in *Crancour Ltd* v. *Merola*,[47] two cases were heard by the court where the landlord brought possession proceedings by issuing an originating summons under R.S.C. Order 113.[48] Under this, summary proceedings for eviction can be instituted where an occupier, who is not a statutory tenant, is in occupation without consent. In both these cases, the defendant occupiers claimed that they had a tenancy and therefore that the proceedings were ill-founded. The agreements in both cases were in identical terms (since Crancour Ltd were successor in title in Mr Markou) and contained the following provisions: (1) the occupier could use the room only between the hours of midnight and 10.30 a.m. and between noon and midnight of each day, (2) the possession, management and control of the room remained vested in the licensor, (3) the licensor provide the following attendance: a housekeeper, lighting, cleaning of common parts, telephone, linen laundry, hot water, etc. The possession proceedings were granted in the County Court whereupon the occupiers appealed. The Court of Appeal held that the judge should not have allowed these proceedings as 'short-cut' proceedings and the case was sent back for a full retrial in order to determine whether or not there was a tenancy. The Court of Appeal, however, did give detailed and useful guidance on how to interpret sham clauses. Ralph Gibson LJ declared:

> The fact that services which the landlord is contractually obliged to provide are not taken or used by the lodger does not render the agreement a sham since the lodger was entitled to call for them. The fact that the landlord had not exercised his right to require the lodger to move to another room also, in the view of the learned judge, could not show the agreement to be a sham. The judge was right ... As to the denial in the agreement signed by the appellants of the right in them as occupiers to use the room from 10.30 to noon, I agree that this clause has the appearance of one which might well be a sham in the sense that the landlord might be shown not to have intended the term to be true statement of the nature of the occupation to be enjoyed by the licensees ... If clauses of such importance are self-evidently of doubtful effectiveness, the court must consider the possibility that the clauses which impose the obligation to provide attendance and reserve the right of control and access for the purpose of providing it may not accurately reflect the legal relationship intended by the parties with reference to those matters.[49]

Nicholls LJ was, however, far more forthright in his condemnation of the clauses in the agreement:

> That (Clause 1) was ever really intended by the original licensor ... strains my credibility too far ... I think that it would be unsatisfactory for summary judgment to be given in favour of a landlord on the strength of a form of written agreement when *prima facie* the basic clause in that agreement is an *artificial contrivance intended to mislead* and thereby intended to create or strengthen a claim by the landlord that the agreement was outside the Rent Acts.[50] (Emphasis added.)

It does seem that after *Street* the courts are now highly suspicious of clauses that have no real relevance to the reality of the arrangement and which are being entered into by both parties to the contract. That being so, the court can move to declaring certain clauses *prima facie* to be shams on the face of the agreement. The underlying purpose, as here, is clearly to protect the status of residential security in an occupant of premises. Clearly, if the courts were not concerned to maintain the application of the Rent Acts they would not be exercising their discretion in this way. As a result, even where a letting shows *ex facie* that the Rent Acts do not apply, the court will now usually reject the possibility of a landlord taking the benefit of a letting without the burden of the Rent Acts as well.

The courts' approach in the above two cases has been stretched even to cases which were clearly not envisaged by *Street*. In *Bretherton* v. *Paton*[51] the occupier went into possession of the landlord's premises and began paying rent to him, whilst at the same time undertaking a renovation of the premises, the house being in a dilapidated condition. In this way, the occupier hoped to put the house back into a good condition before obtaining a mortgage loan to purchase the premises from the landlord. The occupier entered into this agreement with the landlord and began residing in the house. However, he later decided that he would not buy it. Subsequently, the landlord was served with a notice to repair by the local authority and he gave the occupier notice to quit and claimed possession in the County Court. The judge found for the landlord and held that the occupier simply had a licence of the premises. The judge held that the occupation was 'preferable to and forms part of an ineffective arrangement for the sale and purchase of land . . . the inference of a tenancy that would otherwise arise from the exclusive possession of premises at a term for a rent is thereby rebutted'.[52] However, the Court of Appeal reversed this ruling by applying *Street* and holding that the grant of exclusive possession created a tenancy. Yet, in *Street* Lord Templeman had expressly mentioned 'occupancy under a contract for sale of land' as a legal relationship that would negate the grant of an estate or interest even with exclusive possession. The Court of Appeal did not consider this exception to apply. It found that the intention, given the facts of the transaction, was to grant exclusive possession for a term at a rent, and that this brought it under the decision in *Street*:

> These parties entered into an arrangement with the ultimate intention of negotiating a sale. But, to quote the words of Lord Templeman, the intention which was demonstrated by the agreement was 'to grant exclusive possession for a term at a rent' and therefore this case comes clearly within the decision of *Street* v. *Mountford*.[53]

The court would not look at extrinsic evidence outside the terms of the agreement as shedding further light on the parties' intentions. If the court had to do that, it would simply, in the interest of residential security, interpret the agreement in such a way as to make it subject to the provisions of the Rent Acts, thus protecting the status of a tenant in occupation. This case demonstrates vividly how far the courts have been prepared to go after *Street* in protecting the rights of ordinary citizens to residential security and to promote this idea as a public value. The decision emphasizes that the occupier also has legitimate interests, even on such facts as the present, which should be protected through the enforcement of an egalitarian social contract.

Some limitations have, however, been suggested on how far *Street* can be taken. In *Brooker Settled Estates Ltd* v. *Ayres*[54] the Court of Appeal made an important distinction between a lodger and a tenant. Here the occupier took a room in a flat shared with two others. He signed an agreement which defined his occupation as a licence to occupy the flat in common with other licensees. He was given no exclusive possession of any part of the premises. Nevertheless, the County Court held that the occupier was not a lodger. Therefore, he must be a tenant of the premises. In the Court of Appeal, however, it was decided that just because an occupier is not a lodger that does not necessarily make him a tenant. To that extent, the Court limited the application of *Street*. It held that in *Street* exclusive possession had been conceded by the landlord whereas in this case it was the only live factual issue, and yet this was critical. The case was remitted back to the County Court for a retrial on the issue whether the occupier actually had exclusive possession and whether he had a tenancy.[55] This case is not directly relevant to the principle of residential security in the cases. However, it is of importance in demonstrating that the courts still require care to be taken with clauses which are potentially shams or pretences: so much so, that they are prepared to order a retrial. The courts are so adamant in this now that they will refuse to uphold sham clauses even where the landlord advises that the occupier seek legal advice before signing anything.

In *Nicolaou* v. *Pitt*[56] a flat was advertised as being available on licence. Three ladies took the flat. The landlord explained to them the nature of the licence. He advised them to consult a solicitor. A recital in the agreement stated that 'the licensor is not willing to grant the licensee exclusive possession'. Before the end of their term, two of the ladies left the premises and were replaced by another who applied to have a fair rent registered, whereupon the landlord brought possession proceedings. The judge found that there was a tenancy and gave his judgment thus:

> Mr Nicolaou was asked if he seriously had it in contemplation to introduce a third person – a stranger – into the flat. After a certain amount of humming and hawing he said he did so contemplate. I do not believe him. I do not think he ever contemplated introducing either a third person nor himself, occupying the flat. He wanted to get around the Rent Acts . . . Despite the words which were used and despite what was

> said I am satisfied that Mr Nicolaou intended to grant exclusive possession.[57]

The landlord appealed this decision. The Court of Appeal agreed with the judge at first instance. It applied *Street* and emphasized the pre-eminence given to the effect of an agreement rather than its expressed terms. It declared that

> it is not accurate to say that the parties 'agreed' that their relationship should be a licence. They had a joint explicit intention that the agreement should give them their mutual rights and duties of licensors and licensees, *but the categorisation of the agreement as a licence or a tenancy is for the law to decide, not the parties.*[58] (Emphasis added.)

The Court of Appeal continued:

> It matters not that the parties described the agreement as a licence or that the landlord explained that he does not want to grant security of tenure, or indeed that this is accepted. If, in fact, the intention is to grant exclusive possession at a rent. It is that which creates a tenancy.[59]

Here, therefore, the court held a tenancy to have been created by Mr Nicolaou, the landlord. This case is another authority for the proposition that a landlord who derogates from his grant of a tenancy will not be allowed by the courts to escape from his obligations under the Rent Acts. It is clear, then, that the stipulated terms have to serve some clear purpose before they can be accepted by the courts.

In *Aslan* v. *Murphy*,[60] the Court of Appeal decided that clauses restricting or excluding the occupier from the premises at certain times of the day may be regarded as shams if they serve no ostensible purpose. They are then designed merely to prevent the coming into existence of exclusive possession. Under a licence agreement a landlord let a small single room on the basis that 'the licensor is not willing to grant exclusive possession of any part of the room'. The agreement also contained provisions that the licensor would retain a key giving him the absolute right of entry at all times, and that the licensee could only have occupation from midday to midnight and from midnight to 10.30 a.m. When the landlord sought possession proceedings the County Court decided in his favour, even though the occupier argued that the provisions in the agreements were pretences since the room was far too small to share with another and the vacation of the room between 10.30 a.m. and midday was unenforceable. The judge held that 'Mr Aslan made it quite plain that he never intended to grant Mr Murphy exclusive possession of the room for the very good reason that he had been advised that to do so might lead to the creation of a tenancy'. On appeal, the Court of Appeal held that the court below should have examined the entire agreement, but without the pretences. The pretences in this case were the provisions which were designed to prevent exclusive possession from coming into existence when the document was read without the pretences. Lord Donaldson, giving the judgment of the Court, criticized the judge as follows:

> Where he went wrong was in considering whether the whole agreement was a sham, and having concluded that it was not, giving effect to its terms, i.e. taking it throughout at face value. What he should have done . . . was to consider whether the whole agreement was a sham and, if it was not, whether in the light of the factual situation the provisions . . . were part of the true bargain between the parties or were pretences. Both provisions were wholly unrealistic and were clearly pretences.[61]

In explaining why an agreement should not be taken at its face value, but examined in the light of the factual situation, the Court gave an inkling of the policy basis for such an approach and implicitly demonstrated why a pro-residence approach was necessary in the proper application of the law:

> The labels which the parties agreed to attach to themselves or to their agreements are never conclusive and in this particular field in which there is *enormous pressure on the homeless to agree* to any label which will facilitate the obtaining of accommodation, they give no guidance at all.[62] (Emphasis added.)

Once again, it is submitted that the imposition of an egalitarian social contract on the contracting parties is the surest way to neutralize 'the enormous pressure on the homeless to agree to any label', which in the context is the true factual context in which the transactions of the parties take place. Only then can the courts move to equalize the respective position of the parties to the contract.

In *Duke* v. *Wynne*[63] the Court of Appeal once again downplayed the importance of label-attaching and express words in the agreement. Mrs Duke let her former matrimonial home out for two years, as she did not know what to do with it. She signed a licence agreement with the occupier which contained the following two clauses. First, that 'the owner wishes to obtain vacant possession on very short notice and the occupant accepts as a fundamental term and condition of the Agreement that no tenancy is created . . . There is no right of exclusive possession.' Second, that 'the owner shall permit the occupant to have the non-exclusive occupation of the premises and reserves the right to place another person or persons in the premises ... Visitors shall leave by 12 p.m.' Later, however, Mrs Duke decided to emigrate and to sell the house. The Court followed the judgment of the Court of Appeal in *Antoniades*, which was subsequently reversed by the House of Lords, and the judge held that the surrounding circumstances were sufficient to negate a tenancy. The landlord appealed. The Court of Appeal reversed the ruling by the judge and held that there had been exclusive possession, despite the two clauses, and therefore a tenancy had come into existence:

> On the facts in *Aslan* v. *Murphy* it would have been possible for them to have shared the house with another occupant ... However, the evidence did not disclose any immediate intention on the part of Mrs Duke to make such an arrangement, and she never in fact did so ... In the instant appeal it is quite clear that the true bargain was that the Wynnes should be entitled to exclusive possession unless and until Mrs Duke wanted to exercise her right to authorise someone else to move in as a lodger and she never suggested that this was a serious possibility.[64]

Therefore, because the evidence did not disclose an immediate intention to share the premises with another person the true bargain was that Mr Wynne, the occupier, was to have exclusive possession of the premises. Initially, the Court would not allow Mrs Duke, the landlord, to unilaterally change the nature of the contract. Here also, therefore, the Court has been concerned to detect pretences and to follow *Street* and to say that once exclusive possession at a rent for a term is found, a tenancy is the result. This is, of course, a departure from the law of contract to a policy-led approach in judicial decision-making. Yet it is the only way, given the innumerable factual situations and permutations that arise before the courts, to promote justice and consistency in the law. It is also a supreme example of the primacy of personal rights over property rights.

Separate Agreements for Sharing Occupiers

Multiple occupation may come about if people either share premises or have entered into separate agreements. The unfolding scenario can be quite complicated. If each occupier has a tenancy of a separate part of the property, the occupiers may be 'parallel' tenants. Or, they may just be sharing premises as licensees. Or, if not licensees, they may be joint tenants of the whole property. Let us first consider the case of parallel occupation of premises.

In *Hadjiloucas* v. *Crean*[65] two occupiers took separate licences of a two-bedroomed flat. Each was, however, liable also for the rent of the other. One occupier left the flat and was then replaced with the consent of the landlord by another. The landlord then brought possession proceedings when one of the occupiers applied for the registration of a fair rent. The County Court held that as there was no exclusive occupation, the occupiers were licensees, and granted a possession order. The Court of Appeal, however, ordered a retrial and remitted the case back to the County Court to see if the facts justified the finding that there were two separate licences here and not a joint tenancy. In order to do this, the question of exclusive possession had to be looked at. Mustill LJ declared that in *Street*, Lord Templeman could not have intended to convey that,

> for the purpose of deciding a case of the present kind, the judge clearly has to rule out the possibility that the occupier is a lodger to find that the occupation is exclusive, for such reasoning would treat exclusive occupation as the consequence of a tenancy, whereas elsewhere it is made clear that it is a prerequisite.[66]

This appears to be an unsatisfactory judgment for it suggests that it is possible for the occupier to be in exclusive occupation and yet merely to have the rights of a licensee. It is, once again, a severe limitation on the rights created by *Street*. It would appear to be a move away from the protection of residential security. Instead, it tends, once again, to interpret the law in a way that gives considerable flexibility to landlords. Similarly, the interpretation of the court of sham cases appears also to be a misapplication of *Street*. In the words of Purchas LJ,

> Sham cases do envisage the incorporation of a clause by which neither party intends to be bound and which is obviously a smoke-screen to cover the real intentions of both contracting parties: see *Snook*.[67]

In *Street*, the definition of sham was extended by the court to incorporate the appearance of a pretence. The older definition in *Snook* was based upon a reliance on the mutual intention of the parties, which is not wholly real, whereas in *Street* the House of Lords considered the definition of sham to apply equally to cases where it did not concern itself with the mutual intention of the parties. This is a restrictive definition, therefore, of shams. It is once again intended to provide landlords with considerable flexibility in letting out property.

The case of *A. G. Securities* v. *Vaughan*[68] arose later and is, in principle, a better case in the context of multiple lettings. The case was decided in favour of the landlord at first instance, reversed on appeal by the Court of Appeal, and then reversed again by the House of Lords to restore the decision of the County Court judge. Here the argument before the courts was only whether the occupiers were licensees or joint tenants of the whole property, but the possibility of parallel tenancy was not raised. The landlord granted a four-bedroomed flat to four occupiers at different times, taking from each a different agreement, with different monthly rent payments being specified for each grantee. When the landlord subsequently sought possession of the flat the County Court held that the four agreements accurately reflected the nature of the agreement which was to create a licence, and not a tenancy. Fox LJ in the Court of Appeal, however, held[69] that the trial judge had erred in finding separate licences, for the occupiers collectively had exclusive possession, holding as four joint tenants of the whole:

> If one looks at the position as it was when the first to fourth defendants were all in occupation of the flat it seems to me that they had, between them, exclusive possession of the flat. They were entitled to exclude anybody; the plaintiff has no right of entry.[70]

This, however, would appear to be a misconstruction of the law. It is of course true that the landlord had deliberately devised such a scheme in order to prevent the application of the Rent Acts from taking place and the status of residential security from arising in the occupiers. However, to suggest that a joint interest was created here, is to stretch the language. A joint interest only arises if the four unities of time, title, interest and possession are in existence. Here, only the requirement of possession was satisfied. Yet Fox LJ explained the Court of Appeal decision as follows. First, for unity of title there was a 'single implied agreement for the grant of exclusive possession to the defendants and made between the defendants and the plaintiffs at the time when the fourth defendant's agreement was signed. The individual agreements are, no doubt, evidence of the transactions, but it seems to me that the single implied agreement is what finally brings the relationship into being.' Second, for unity of time the joint tenancy arose by implication when the fourth defendant's agreement was signed, and no sooner, so the earlier signing of the first to the third defendants' agreements was superseded. Third, for unity of interest each agreement lasted for six months, even though signed at different times, and thereafter were determinable on one month's notice. Therefore, the determinability on notice was identical for each of the occupiers and did not disrupt the joint nature of the holding. The unity of interest was not disrupted either by the different rent that was payable, nor was it disrupted by the fact that there was no evidence to suggest that each occupant was liable jointly for the rent of others, which would normally be a requirement for a joint tenancy.[71] If the Court of Appeal is right in these respects, then all that is normally required for the finding of a joint tenancy is multiple occupation with the finding of collective exclusive occupation. This is a very liberal interpretation of a joint tenancy. It runs contrary to orthodoxy.[72]

It is submitted that this is the kind of radical departure from established legal principles through the exercise of judicial discretion that we saw in Lord Denning's judgment in *Bull* v. *Bull* in Chapter 1. The underlying purpose has been the same: to do justice. There the Court of Appeal was seeking to ensure that, on the basis of an egalitarian social contract, an ungrateful son should not turn out his mother from her home, just because he can rely on legal principles. Here, the Court is concerned to show, again through the application of the egalitarian social contract, that landlords in a superior bargaining position should not use the weight of the law to divest occupiers in their property of the benefits of residential security of tenure. In both cases, the courts have adapted the law with a view to achieving these ends. Yet there is a difficulty with the Court of Appeal's approach in the latter case. If all letting of premises in multiple occupation will create joint tenancies in this way then all will stand to become protected tenancies. The difficulty with this is that it does not just put in place mechanisms to prevent landlords from making unfair decisions. It actually changes the substantive content of the law. Sir George Waller dissented from the majority judgment arguing that there were four distinct licences here and 'to try to make into a joint tenancy would be to create a wholly artificial situation'.[73]

The House of Lords agreed.[74] Their Lordships held that the agreements were not shams but reflected the true situation of no exclusive possession. If a licensee died, the landlord had the right to introduce another licensee and the *jus accrescendi* was excluded by the contractual terms. The agreements simply could not give rise to one joint interest. Yet, Lord Oliver did recognize the basis behind the reasoning of the Court of Appeal which was to prevent landlords from having recourse to ingenious devices which would defeat the wide-ranging attempts connected to social reform in the Rent Acts. This commitment was designed, through the agency of the law, to give equal protection to tenants just as landlords had before. As Lord Oliver explained,

> [S]ince lettings of residential property of an appropriate rateable value attract the consequences of controlled rent and security of tenure provided by the Rent Acts, it is not, perhaps, altogether surprising that those who derive their income from residential property are constantly seeking to attain the not always reconcilable objectives on the one hand of keeping their property gainfully occupied and, on the other, of framing their contractual arrangements with the occupants in such a way as to avoid, if they can, the application of the Acts. Since it is only a letting which attracts the operation of the Acts, such endeavours normally take the form of entering into contractual arrangements designed, on their face, to ensure that no estate is created in the occupant for the time being and that his occupation of the land derives merely from a personal and revocable permission granted by way of licence. The critical question, however, in every case is not simply how the arrangement is presented to the outside world in the relevant documentation, but what is the true nature of the arrangement.[75]

However, having defined the problem in this way the House of Lords rejected the Court of Appeal's liberal interpretation of the Rent Acts. Whereas the trend to the application of the Rent Acts to sole occupiers was to be firmly welcomed, it was not to be welcomed in its application to multiple occupants if that involved a fundamental redefinition of joint interests.[76] It is, of course, a moot point whether the House of Lords should have extended the ambit of Rent Act protection to multiple occupation cases as well.

In *Antoniades* v. *Villiers*[77] the question of multiple occupation rose again, once more demonstrating the ever-present difficulties of construction in this area. A young couple who were living together as man and wife inspected a flat together and decided to take it. When it came to drawing up the contractual arrangements, each was asked by the landlord to sign a separate licence agreement and this was done by each contemporaneously. Under the licence agreement exclusive possession was not granted. However, the couple had asked for a double bed to be placed in their room; there was never any question that they were seeking to establish a joint home, and they were the sole occupants of the flat at all times. Yet clause 16 of the agreements went on to state that 'the licensor shall be entitled at any time to use the rooms together with the licensee and permit other persons to use of the rooms together with the licensee'. When the occupiers applied for a fair rent to be registered the landlord brought possession proceedings in the County Court, which were denied, whereupon he appealed.

In the Court of Appeal[78] judgment was given for the landlord. The occupiers claimed that clause 16 was a sham or a pretence. However, the Court of Appeal held that for there to be a sham it was necessary to prove that both the landlord and tenant intended that the clause would be a sham. The landlord did not intend to grant exclusive possession. Clause 16 was not a sham. The agreements created two separate licences and no exclusive possession was granted. The court accepted the definition of a sham given by Purchas LJ in *Hadjiloucas* v. *Crean*, which Bingham LJ summarized as whenever 'the parties say one thing intending another'. Bingham LJ held that the agreement was not a smokescreen to cover the real intentions of both contracting parties. He asked two questions: (1) on what grounds, if one party had left the premises, could the remaining party have been made liable for anything more than the £87 which he or she had agreed to pay? and (2) on what grounds could they have resisted a demand by the respondent to introduce a further person into the premises? But in following the definition of a sham in *Hadjiloucas*, which in itself followed from the classic definition in *Snook*, Bingham LJ was inevitably following the narrow definition and not the broader one handed down by the House of Lords in *Street*. He continued:

> If the written agreements are to be discarded as a sham it must be shown not only that the occupants intended to enjoy a right to exclusive possession but also that the landlord shared that intention. In my view he plainly did not. He was determined that they should not enjoy that right. Doubtless his determination was conditioned by his desire that the relationship between himself and the occupants should not be governed by the Rent Acts, but that intention must be understood as fortifying rather than undermining his intention that the occupants should have no right to exclusive possession.[79]

However, in the House of Lords,[80] Lord Templeman took quite a different view – and quite as credibly – thus demonstrating how difficult and policy-orientated this area of the law is. Whereas Bingham LJ's view could be put forward quite plausibly on the facts, given His Lordship's rigorous analysis, it could also be rejected plausibly by the House of Lords if the law was intended to do something quite different in this case. Was the purpose of the law to prevent resourceful landlords from drafting documents that would have the effect of denying residential security to occupants or was it to reward them, in a free-market economy, for their ingenuity in these circumstances? Lord Templeman had no doubt that the separate signed documents here had to be read as one, so that

> the real transaction was, as the judge (at first instance) found, one under which the appellants became joint tenants with exclusive possession, on the footing that the two agreements are to be construed together ... it would follow that they were together jointly and severally responsible for the whole rent. It would equally follow that they could effectively exclude the respondent and his nominees.

The documents could not be read separately and this is why they were a sham for

> there is an air of total unreality about these documents read as separate and individual licences in the light of the circumstance that all the appellants were together seeking a flat as a quasi-matrimonial home ... nor in the circumstances can any realistic significance be given to clauses 16 and 17 of the document. It cannot realistically have been contemplated that the respondent would either himself use or occupy any part of the flat or put some other person in to share accommodation specifically adapted for the occupation by a couple living together. These clauses cannot be considered as seriously intended to have any practical operation or to serve any purpose apart from the purely technical one of seeking to avoid the ordinary legal consequences attendant upon letting the appellants into possession at a monthly rent.

Lord Templeman also held that the definition of a sham in *Hadjiloucas*, which was followed by Bingham LJ, should be rejected as too narrow. In his view, any provision should be struck out if it is not intended to be relied upon. It would be a sham in that it would be an unlawful attempt to contract out of the Rent Acts. This expansive redefinition of a sham must be seen as an undisguised attempt to put policy before freedom of contract. This is abundantly clear from Lord Templeman's tenant-orientated stance:

> Parties to an agreement cannot contract out of the Rent Acts; if they were able to do so the Acts would be a dead letter because in a state of housing shortage a person seeking residential accommodation may agree to anything to obtain shelter. The Rent Acts protect a tenant but they do not protect a licensee. Since parties to an agreement cannot

> contract out of the Rent Acts, a document which expresses the intention, genuine or bogus, of both parties or of one party to create a licence will nevertheless create a tenancy if the rights and obligations enjoyed and imposed satisfy the legal requirements of a tenancy. A person seeking residential accommodation may concur in any expression of intention in order to obtain shelter. Since parties to an agreement cannot contract out of the Rent Acts, a document expressed in the language of a licence must nevertheless be examined and construed by the court in order to decide whether the rights and obligations enjoyed and imposed create a licence or a tenancy. A person seeking residential accommodation may sign a document couched in any language in order to obtain shelter. Since parties to an agreement cannot contract out of the Rent Acts, the grant of a tenancy to two persons jointly cannot be concealed, accidentally or by design, by the creation of two documents in the form of licences.[81]

This is a very clear-cut case of the importance of policy in judicial decision-making. The policy basis is clear as much in the Court of Appeal as it is in the House of Lords. In both cases the policy premises can be put forward quite logically and credibly. But there is no mistake about it: it is just as much a policy decision to say that a landlord who is determined that his occupants should not have their rights governed by the Rent Acts can succeed in his design, provided that he can show that he did not intend to give them exclusive possession (Bingham LJ), as it is to say that parties to an agreement cannot contract out of the Rent Acts, because to do so would turn them into a dead letter in the current state of housing shortage. To recognize this is not in any way to disregard the constitutional duty of the courts which is always to enforce the letter of parliamentary Acts. Put another way, the courts can do their constitutional duty and yet exercise powerful policy preferences.

The egalitarian approach arising from Lord Oliver's recognition of the importance of the Rent Acts in *A. G. Securities* was given support by Buckley LJ in *Stribling* v. *Wickham*[82] who urged an even-handed approach to the consideration of the question whether a transaction is, or contains, a pretence and whether such a pretence is designedly undertaken in order to evade the Rent Acts. New occupants of a flat signed three separate agreements, with identical 'licence fees' to be payable in each case. Each document purported to create a licence and each included the recital: 'whereas the licensor is not willing to grant the licencee exclusive possession of any part of the premises . . . and is anxious to secure the use of the premises notwithstanding that such use be in common with the licensor and such other licencees and invitees as the licensor may permit.' Before the term ended, two of the occupiers moved out. They were replaced by new occupiers on identical terms. When the landlord sought possession against all the occupiers, they claimed collectively to have exclusive possession and to be joint tenants of the flat. The Recorder, applying *A. G. Securities* in the Court of Appeal, found that there was a joint tenancy and declined to make an order for the possession for the landlord.

On appeal, the Court of Appeal had regard to the House of Lords decision in *A. G. Securities*, which had by then been decided, and reversed the decision of the Recorder. The House of Lords had in that case ruled out a 'flexible' approach to the determination of a joint tenancy. The constituent elements of a tenancy were missing here and the arrangement could only be properly categorized as being three separate licence agreements, none of which could have individually conferred exclusive possession. As the Court of Appeal held:

> The flat was suitable for use by a multiple but shifting population ... (on leaving one of the licencees) makes it plain that he was intending to terminate his own rights and obligations only, and that the positions of the other two would be unaffected ... In my judgment, there is no process of 'legal alchemy' by which the agreements can be placed in to the mould of a tenancy ... The three licences were in substance and reality just what they purported to be ... They cannot be ignored nor can they be converted by any legitimate purpose into a joint obligation to pay the whole rent or a form of authority to each occupant by the others to terminate a joint tenancy on notice by him, but by some magical process to re-create on the instant a joint tenancy in the remaining two until expiry of the current agreements.[83]

Thus, the Court has followed *A. G. Securities* in the House of Lords with the result that there is now far less likelihood of collective exclusive possession being recognized to bring the cases on multiple occupation within the protection of the Rent Acts. The Court requires full satisfaction that the four unities, as traditionally defined in the orthodox doctrine, have to be shown to exist for joint ownership.

Yet, it is important to recognize that *A. G. Securities* is not without limitation and can be distinguished. This happened in *Mikeover Ltd* v. *Brady*[84] where the Court of Appeal held that a joint tenancy could not be created where two identical agreements conferred on the occupiers a joint right of exclusive occupation because each licensee had to pay part only of the rent, thereby indicating that the obligation of one licensee was entirely independent of the obligation of the other. The landlord offered a two-bedroomed flat for two people to share. It was agreed that the flat was only suitable for two people who were 'mutually acceptable'. Two occupiers took the flat and signed separate agreements. Clause 1 read: 'the owner grants to the licensee the right to use the flat in common with others who have been granted the like right.' When one occupier moved out before the end of the term the other continued to pay his part of the rent only. No other licensees were introduced. Arrears in rent began to arise and the landlord obtained a possession order from a County Court judge who held that he had properly determined the licence.

This was upheld on appeal by the Court of Appeal. Once again the judgment of the House of Lords in *A. G. Securities* was followed. Consequently, the Court adopted a strict definition of the joint tenancy, with the requirement of a joint obligation to pay the entire rent, which was absent here. The liability, however, here was entirely independent and several and there was no unity of interest. In the words of Slade LJ, the occupier 'offered to pay monthly sums of one hundred and seventy three pounds and thirty two pence (the single rent per person being eighty six pounds and sixty six pence) but, as the judge found, (the landlord) refused this offer saying "I can't accept it. I'll hold you responsible for your share only"'.[85] One might ask whether there is any rational reason for the continuing tendency to exclude small groups of occupiers from the protection of the Rent Acts, when sole occupiers would have protection of those laws under the same contracts. Surely, if there are legitimate rights in the case of sole occupiers then there are legitimate rights also in the case of pairs of occupiers or small groups of occupiers that are equally deserving of legal protection.

The failing in the law, it is submitted, is the direct result of a failure to think conceptually about the protection accorded to legitimate property rights. If citizens have rights deserving of equal protection, then it matters not whether the citizen is renting property individually or with a group, whom he may not know, and all of whom may sign separate letting agreements. In fact, in large cities and in areas of acute housing shortage, it is more likely for single people to be renting on precisely this basis. Should not the court, then, be extending protection to groups of such people on the basis of an imposed social contract between the landlord and the occupiers of those premises? Further, is it not false to deny existence of collective exclusive possession here, when on the same facts sole exclusive possession would be proved if there had only been one written agreement between the parties?

Yet protection of group occupiers was strongly advocated by

Fox LJ and the majority of the Court of Appeal in *A. G. Securities*. The majority there found that the attributes of a joint tenancy could all be shown by implication where there is a simultaneous surrender and a re-grant of all the existing occupiers' licences whenever a new occupier joined the group. The traditional joint tenancy could thereby be expanded to meet the emerging needs of modern society, while at the same time serving traditional purposes. However, in this way the courts could define exclusive possession and locate a tenancy even though the four occupiers moved in at different times, paid different rents and signed separate contracts. Yet, through this modification the number of tenancies that are statutorily protected would increase in accordance with the social goal of the Rent Acts. Some support for this is seen in the earlier case of *Demuren* v. *Seal Estates* where the Court of Appeal found a joint tenancy notwithstanding a severed rent obligation. In the words of Megaw LJ, there was no logical inconsistency in discovering a joint tenancy here because there was 'the provision of post-dated cheques the effect of which is that the landlord has got his payment in advance up to (the end of the term) from each of the two applicants'.[86] It is regrettable that these isolated developments are not encouraged and given endorsement by the House of Lords in *A. G. Securities*. In the event, multiple occupation of premises under separate agreements is not protected by the Rent Acts. Clearly, an equalitarian approach grounded in principles of citizenship should be adopted in such cases.

Local Authority Occupancies

Finally in this chapter we consider the effect of *Street* in the context of Local Authority housing. In *Eastleigh B.C.* v. *Walsh*,[87] the occupant was offered housing under the Housing (Homeless Persons) Act 1977 from his local Council. He signed a receipt for the keys which read 'these keys relate to my tenancy', and received a document with the heading 'Conditions of Tenancy' which contained the following terms: (1) the tenancy could be terminated by four weeks' notice; and (2) acceptance of the tenancy would be conclusive evidence of agreement to the terms. As he was about to assume occupation of the premises, his wife and children left him, but he neglected to tell the Council of this. When this was discovered, he was given notice to quit and the Council brought possession proceedings in the County Court. The judge held that, despite the wording of the agreement, the Council had only offered a licence of the premises, since 'Parliament never intended or expected that what was obviously temporary accommodation should be intended to be a tenancy so that all the protection of the law followed'.[88] The reason why this grant of premises by the Council was intended to be temporary was because the Council, at the time of the grant, was still undertaking enquiries about whether or not there was a priority need here. On appeal the Court of Appeal accepted that the Council was not subject to the burden of the Rent Acts in this case. Yet this was the case where exclusive possession of the premises had been offered. On the face of it, the House of Lords judgment in *Street* should have applied. However, Griffiths LJ held that:

> In my view the judge was entitled to look at this arrangement with the eyes of common sense and to conclude as he did that a Council giving emergency shelter under this Act was not intending to create a tenancy . . . and that he was further entitled to draw the inference that the occupant well realised that was the true state of affairs.[89]

The House of Lords, however, reversed the ruling of the Court of Appeal on the basis that

> [t]he appellant was granted exclusive possession of the house on terms which are fully set out in the contemporaneous documents, viz. the authority's offer of a tenancy . . . the appellant's acceptance . . . and the document entitled 'Conditions of Tenancy' . . . Reading these unambiguous documents in the light of (the Housing (Homeless Persons) Act 1977) I can see no ground for any finding that the 'nature of the occupancy of the house by the appellant was as licensee and not as tenant'.[90]

To conclude, even though this was a rather unmeritorious applicant, the House of Lords simply applied the recently clarified rules of the House as to the existence of a tenancy in particular circumstances. According to these rules, the fact of exclusive possession was the decisive factor here. Barring the existence of any shams, the court made a finding of a tenancy here because this is what was intended when the documents were signed and when exclusive possession of the premises was given to the occupant. This case suggests that the ability of a landlord to avoid the Rent Acts after *Street* is now considerably limited unless, for example, the landlord were to let residential premises with services, in which case this would fall under one of the categories of exclusive possession which were specifically excepted from becoming a tenancy under the rules laid down by the Lords in *Street*. This case also suggests that once exclusive possession has been granted it will now be very difficult to rebut it by extrinsic evidence.

The House of Lords judgment in *Street* was applied in the context of the provision of accommodation by local authorities, pursuant to their duties under the Housing Act 1985 in relation to homeless persons, in the case of *Ogwr B.C.* v. *Dykes*[91] also. A family in council housing was sent a letter by the Council that the house was provided to them under the Council's duty under the 1977 Act, and that their occupation was by way of licence for thirteen weeks, to allow them reasonable opportunity to secure permanent accommodation elsewhere. The Council did not, however, seek possession proceedings until about a year later when it gave the family notice to terminate the licence and applied to the County Court. The judge at first instance held that the Council had validly determined the licence and this was upheld by the Court of Appeal, which held that even where the three elements of a lease, as defined in *Street*, were in existence there could still be the inference of a licence. The exceptions were specifically mentioned in *Street* as including an occupier who was a trespasser, for example. The Court of Appeal held that the stated list of exceptions in *Street* was not exhaustive. It held that the context of the grant can be critical:

> The contract under which occupation is granted must be construed objectively and of course, as appears from the authorities to which I have referred (viz. *Street*, *Hadjiloucas*, *A. G. Securities*), this does not mean necessarily according to the express words included in the documents. If all that is disclosed is the granting of exclusive possession for a fixed term for the payment of a rental fee then, in the absence of any feature indicating the contrary, the intention of the parties as expressed by their agreement must be to create a tenancy. If, however, the context in which the right to exclusive possession is granted specifically and definitively negatives an intention to create a tenancy, then some other interest appropriate to the intention established by that context will be created.[92]

The Court of Appeal here is acting contrary to the judgment in *Bretherton* v. *Paton*[93] where it was held that one must not look beyond the document. This decision also does not sit happily with the same Court's judgment in *Eastleigh Borough Council (B.C.)*[94] that we have discussed above. It is submitted that it was far better to have defended this decision on the basis of a common sense approach to short-term emergency housing for the homeless, than to have attempted to defend it by recourse to a dubious principle. At any rate, this case shows that residential security will not be strictly enforced against a Council if there are external circumstances to indicate that the purpose behind the letting was to provide short-term emergency housing. It is not reconcilable with the *Eastleigh B.C.* case, and as such it exhibits a different value-preference by a differently constituted court.

The application of the principles in *Street*, in the context of Local Authority housing under the Housing Act 1985, continued in the case of *Family Housing Association* v. *Jones*.[95] The defendant applied to the Local Council for housing as a homeless person. The Family Housing Association (FHA) of the Council licensed her and her son to occupy a self-contained flat for temporary accommodation and the agreement expressed this to be a licence, without exclusive possession. The FHA retained the key to the premises. When the occupier was offered a new flat elsewhere she refused, whereupon the FHA initiated possession proceedings in the County Court against her. The judge held that neither in law nor in fact was there exclusive possession enjoyed by the defendant:

> Firstly, there was no exclusive possession: because of the nature of the transaction the accommodation was granted on a temporary basis, the landlord retained control by restricting the occupation by the defendant and her son, and the contract contained an express and genuine agreement that exclusive possession was not granted. Further, the landlord in fact retained a key to the premises not as matter of convenience but as a means of free entry to the relevant premises at will . . . This was a refuge, a hostel for homeless people outwith the world of landlords and tenants. There was no exclusive possession, no defined term, occupation could be given up without notice: furthermore there were here exceptional circumstances in the very nature of the transaction which negatived a tenancy.[96]

This conclusion, albeit well thought out and reasoned, was reversed by the Court of Appeal which held that the retention of the keys did not necessarily negate exclusive possession. Balcombe LJ found that the accommodation charge was in fact a weekly rent; payment in advance prevented the FHA determining accommodation before the end of the week; and the clause denying exclusive possession was 'as much a label as is the reference to a "licence" in the same clause and, to use Lord Templeman's spade/fork analogy, cannot prevent the agreement creating a tenancy if that is its true effect'.[97]

Indeed, not only did the Court of Appeal on the same facts find there to be *de jure* a tenancy, but it also found there to be in existence *de facto* a tenancy:

> This was a self-contained flat, and it is clear that Mrs Jones

> and Nicolas were to be its only occupants. Mrs Jones paid a weekly charge for her right to occupy the flat. Thus the agreement fulfills all the requirements which Lord Templeman . . . indicates as being appropriate for the creation of a tenancy.[98]

Balcombe LJ proceeded to distinguish this case from the other Local Authority Housing case of *Ogwr B.C.* v. *Dykes* and commented that

> one of the reasons given in *Ogwr B.C.* v. *Dykes* for holding that the agreement created a licence rather than a tenancy was that the Council was acting under its statutory duty. On this basis the present case is distinguishable, since the FHA was under no such duty . . . In my view, *Ogwr B.C.* v. *Dykes* cannot be reconciled with the subsequent decision of the House of Lords in *A. G. Securities* v. *Vaughan*.[99]

Slade LJ, for his part, observed that there were exceptional categories given in *Street* where an occupier might not be a tenant even though occupation was exclusive, and pointed out that this case had 'special features', namely, the authority of the FHA to use the properties only as temporary housing accommodation for homeless persons referred to it, the nature of the premises being described as temporary housing accommodation, there being a charitable element in the arrangement, and the advice and support Mrs Jones (the occupier) received whilst in the premises. His Lordship went on:

> . . . it may at least be difficult for bodies charged with responsibilities for the housing of the homeless to enter into any arrangement pursuant to section 65(2) of the Housing Act 1985[100] under which the person housed is to enjoy exclusive occupation of the premises, however temporary, without conferring on that person security of tenure . . . I am not sure that this result will inure to the benefit of the class of homeless persons in this country viewed as a whole.[101]

Slade LJ, therefore, had reservations about conferring security of tenure upon an occupier in the context of Local Authority housing. However, he gave a concurring judgment with that of Balcombe LJ because he felt bound by the decisions in *Street* and *Eastleigh B.C.*

This case does demonstrate the concern over security of residential status that different judges have. It is a case where the well reasoned findings of the trial judge have been reversed on appeal, largely as a result of the policy laid down by the House of Lords in *Street*. Yet it has to be remembered that the trial judge expressly found that the retention of the key was not undertaken as a matter of convenience by the Local Authority. It was undertaken to give the Authority unrestricted access. This would clearly then have negated exclusive possession. These decisions cannot, therefore, be rationalized as an application of *Street* alone. They can be rationalized as the application of an egalitarian social contract to the transacting parties. Homeless persons are still homeless whether they come for shelter to the Local Authority or to private landlords. If their vulnerability is to be recognized in the context of private lettings, it should be possible to recognize it in the context of public housing. Citizenship requires nothing less.

Conclusion

In this area, the courts have been faced with promoting or opposing two different sets of values. On the one hand, they have been faced with the economic market which treats property as a commodity, and this ideology of market competition began developing in the early 1970s. On the other hand, they have been faced with the egalitarian response to market competition which sees people's current consumption choices and patterns being determinable by economic and social pressures. In cases like *Aldrington Garages* judicial expression has been given to the first of these values. Geoffrey Lane LJ said that 'if the parties succeed in producing an agreement which, in all the circumstances of the case, is in fact a licence and not a tenancy, they should not be perverted from that course by the Courts . . . ' and Roskill LJ said that 'no doubt the agreements entered into in this case can be said to be a device to avoid the operation of the Rent Acts, but that does not mean that this, or any other Court, must refuse to give effect to them . . . '. In *Street*, however, a diametrically opposed view, giving vent to the second of these values, has been espoused upholding the egalitarian social contract. As Lord Templeman said: 'Parties to an agreement cannot contract out of the *Rent Acts*; if they were able to do so the Acts would be a dead letter because in a state of housing shortage a person seeking residential accommodation may agree to anything, to obtain shelter.' This is a view based on parity and equity for all the community's members. It has the effect of integrating people who exist on the margins of society into the mainstream of communal life. The impact of this value-choice by the Courts has been so great that it has been extended in a case such as *Walsh* to Local Authority housing, even where as Griffiths LJ said, looking at it 'with the eyes of common sense' this was intended to be 'emergency shelter' and not intended to create a tenancy. It is clear that for contemporary citizenship concerns the notion of justice needs to be redefined in the light of the requirements of equity in the law.

Notes and References

1 The Rent Acts have a history of over 70 years in this country. The first Rent Act, the Increase of Rent and Mortgage Interest (War Restrictions) Act, was passed in 1915 as a temporary measure during wartime emergency. The Rent Acts are a social legislation *par excellence* in that they impose a measure of social control in the private sector over the renting out of property by landlords and restrict their freedom of contract in the housing market. Today the protective code for tenants is for the most part contained in Rent Act 1977, and the Housing Act 1980 extended the protection of the Rent Act to public-sector tenants. Lord Scarman has defended the policy of the Rent Acts by stating that he found 'nothing illogical or surprising in parliament legislation to override a property right, if it be thought to be socially necessary'. (See *Davis* v. *Johnson* [1979] AC 264, p. 348.) In his words the 'policy of the Rent Acts was and is to protect the tenant in his home, whether the threat be to extort a premium for the grant or renewal of his tenancy, to increase his rent, or to evict him ... The Rent Acts have throughout their history constituted an interference with contract and property rights for a specific purpose – the redress of the balance of advantage enjoyed in a world of housing shortage by the landlord over those who have to rent their homes.' (See *Horford Investments Ltd* v. *Lambert* [1976] Ch. 39, p. 52.) Lord Denning put it more pithily when he said that 'the guiding light through the darkness of the Rent Acts is to remember that they confer personal security on a tenant in respect of his home'. (See *Feyereisel* v. *Turnidge* [1952] 2 QB 29, p. 37.) Today, however, the Housing Act 1988 has replaced the Rent Act in the private rental sector and has restricted the protection to the tenant in his home.

2 The distinction here is between 'assured' tenants and licensees, but the protection afforded to tenants is a limited one.

3 [1970] 2 QB 657; also [1970] 2 All ER 483.

4 [1970] 2 QB 657, p. 669B.

5 [1978] 2 All ER 993.

6 Section 2(1)(b.b.b) of the Rent Act 1968 as amended by Section 2(1) of the Rent Act 1974 reads that 'a tenancy is not a protected tenancy if ... (b.b.b) the purpose of the tenancy is to confer on the tenant the right to occupy the dwelling house for a holiday'.

7 See judgment of Pennycuick J, p. 997d.

8 *Ibid.*, p. 998g–j.

9 [1974] 1 All ER 131, p. 139.

10 [1977] 1 WLR 1181.

11 *Ibid.*, p. 1185.

12 [1978] 1 WLR 1014.

13 *Ibid.*, p. 1025.

14 *Ibid.*, p. 1027.

15 [1979] 37 P & CR 461.

16 *Ibid.*, p. 468.

17 *Ibid.*, p. 473.
18 (1979) 250 EG 1783.
19 See Stephenson LJ, p. 1086 (quoting the County Court judge).
20 *Ibid.*, p. 1087.
21 *Ibid.*
22 (1979) 249 EG 440.
23 *Ibid.*, p. 441.
24 *Ibid.*
25 (1980) *New Law Journal* (130) 939, p. 941.
26 (1984) 269 EGLR 846.
27 *Ibid.*, p. 850.
28 *Loc. cit.*
29 (1984) 272 EG 326.
30 *Ibid.*, p. 329.
31 *Ibid.*
32 [1985] AC 809.
33 See the Court of Appeal's decision at [1985] 49 P & CR 324, p. 329 (per Slade LJ).
34 *Supra*, note 26.
35 *Supra*, note 15.
36 See the Court of Appeal decision, *op. cit.*, p. 329.
37 *Ibid.*, pp. 329–30.
38 See the House of Lords judgment at [1985] AC 809, pp. 816–18.
39 *Ibid.*, p. 825.
40 *Ibid.*, pp. 826–7.
41 *Ibid.*, p. 819.
42 Tromans, Stephen (1985) Leases and licences in the Lords. *Cambridge Law Journal*, p. 351.
43 *Supra*, note 15.
44 *Supra*, note 29.
45 [1967] 2 QB 786, p. 802.
46 Bright, Steven (1991) Beyond sham and into pretence. *Oxford Journal of Legal Studies* (11), p. 136.
47 [1986] 52 P & CR 204.
48 This Order reads as follows: 'where a person claims possession of land which he alleges is occupied solely by a person or persons (not being a tenant or tenants holding over after the termination of a tenancy) who entered into or remained in occupation without his licence or consent or that of any predecessor in title of his, the proceedings may be brought by originating summons in accordance with the provisions of this Order.'
49 *Ibid.*, p. 215.
50 *Ibid.*, p. 224.
51 (1986) 1 EGLR 172.
52 *Ibid.*
53 *Ibid.*
54 (1987) 1 EGLR 50.
55 See judgment of O'Connor LJ, p. 52.
56 (1989) 1 EGLR 84.

57 *Ibid.*, p. 491.
58 *Ibid.*, p. 492 (per Mustill LJ).
59 *Ibid.*, p. 491.
60 (Nos 1 and 2) [1990] 1 WLR 760.
61 *Ibid.*, p. 772H.
62 *Ibid.*, p. 770D.
63 [1990] 1 WLR 766.
64 *Ibid.*, p. 775H (per Lord Donaldson).
65 [1988] 1 WLR 1006.
66 *Ibid.*, p. 1022D.
67 *Ibid.*, p. 1013F.
68 [1990] 1 AC 417.
69 [1988] 2 All ER 173.
70 *Ibid.*, p. 697H.
71 *Ibid.*, p. 700 (per Fox LJ).
72 In a joint tenancy each of the co-owners is wholly entitled to the whole of a single interest in the land. As Lord Browne-Wilkinson explained in *Hammersmith and Fulham Lbc* v. *Monk* (1992) 1 AC 478, p. 492, if there is a transfer of land to two or more persons as joint tenants this code operates so as to make them, *vis-à-vis* the outside world, one single owner. Joint tenants do not have specific shares in the land.
73 *Ibid.*, p. 704H.
74 [1990] 1 AC 417.
75 *Ibid.*, p. 466F–H.
76 *Ibid.*, pp. 469–70. Also see the judgment of Lord Templeman, pp. 454–66.
77 [1990] 1 AC 417.
78 [1988] 2 All ER 309.
79 *Ibid.*, p. 317h.
80 [1990] 1 AC 417, pp. 454–66 (per Lord Templeman).
81 *Ibid.*, pp. 458–9.
82 (1989) 2 EGLR 35.
83 *Ibid.*, p. 390.
84 [1989] 3 All ER 618.
85 *Ibid.*, p. 621g.
86 (1979) EGLR 440, p. 443.
87 [1985] 1 WLR 525.
88 *Ibid.*, p. 530A.
89 *Ibid.*, p. 530C–E.
90 *Ibid.*, p. 530G–H (per Lord Bridge).
91 [1989] 1 WLR 295.
92 *Ibid.*, p. 302G–H (per Purchas LJ).
93 (1986) 1 EGLR 172, noted *supra*, note 51.
94 *Supra*, note 87.
95 [1990]s 1 WLR 779.
96 *Ibid.*, p. 788C–F (quoted by Balcombe LJ).
97 *Ibid.*, p. 788H.
98 *Loc. cit.*
99 *Ibid.*, p. 789F–G.

100 This brings into effect the duty of the Local Authority to house a homeless person under Section 65(1) of the Housing Act 1985 by stating that 'where they (i.e. the Local Authority) are satisfied that he (i.e. the applicant) has a priority need and are not satisfied that he became homeless intentionally, they shall, unless they notify another Local Housing Authority in accordance with Section 67, ensure that accommodation becomes available for his occupation'.

101 *Supra*, note 95, p. 793E.

Epilogue

[A]ll property . . . is derived directly or indirectly from the government, and held subject to those general regulations, which are necessary to the common good and general welfare –
Chief Justice Lemuel Shaw (US Supreme Court)

Judges cannot ignore policy. Judges do not ignore policy. Judges, indeed, fully avail themselves of policy when they make hard choices. In this study, ranging over a consideration of 'Mortgages and co-owners', 'Bankruptcy and insolvency', and 'Landlords and tenants', we have, in a case-by-case study, seen how decisively important policy preferences can be for judges. These policy considerations, we now know, can range from the tacit, but hardly concealed, assumption that the economic market should be the organizing model for human relations in our society to the view – more often expressly articulated because it is so rare – that markets often fail when operating without regulation, particularly for those who are aged, poor, or otherwise most vulnerable. Judges remain, however, less well decided on what should be the preferred judicial policy of the Courts. What we do know from this study is that, more and more, and at the highest levels, they are beginning to confront questions of social justice, rather than give preference to 'monied might' – to use Lord Denning's earlier phrase. So how can they best develop a policy of judicial decision-making in this crucial, but much neglected, area of social and economic activity?

Judges, it is respectfully submitted, should think in terms of citizenship rights, not as political or economic rights but as fundamentally social rights of community, particularly where they are dealing with homes and homelessness. Citizenship has only come into vogue as an idea in British society in the late 1990s. In the 1930s, T. H. Marshall saw citizenship not only as a political matter, of a status attaching to full membership of a community, but as being associated with equal rights and duties. This is the contemporary meaning of citizenship today. But the social inequality of classes in a market economy has a direct bearing on the practical ability of individuals to exercise citizenship rights as full members of a civic society. So judges can address the fact that citizenship does not *per se* guarantee rights. While property has been critical to full citizenship rights, full property rights – such as of ownership of a home – are not in practice known to be a critical right for all who claim to be full citizens of the state. It is the judges, making the final decisions, who must make the hard choices, who must decide whether or not to engage in a socially integrative process when making those decisions, with less respect for property and more for citizenship rights, defined as the equal access to equal rights.

One way in which they can do this is to make a determined use of a variation of the 'Brandeis Brief' as used in the US and as discussed in Chapter 3. They can justify this technique by viewing all property as a 'social trust', symbolic of an egalitarian social contract between the controller and the claimant of property. The social trust comprises the three components of the recognition of individual rights and interests, the recognition that those having equal rights are not necessarily equally situated in society, and the recognition of the role of the law in achieving a fair resolution of competing interests. Judges should squarely face up to the role of wealthy financial institutions that control the distribution of property in society and they should inquire as to how this serves the public interst in given specific cases. This does not necessarily mean stifling the role of the economic market in social behaviour. It does mean evaluating it with a view to achieving greater social justice than has hitherto been the case. Courts can then decide how best to exercise such under-used discretions as the Section 30 discretion of the Law of Property Act 1925. The tool of the 'Brandeis Brief' can be used to work out precisely what really is an act of social justice and in the public interest. In hard policy choice areas as the Law of Landlord and Tenant or Bankruptcy and Insolvency, it would greatly assist the judges to have empirical evidence at hand pointing to the effects of particular social and economic practices. In this way their policy choices can be informed not by dry technical concepts 'in these cold courts' – to use a phrase by Atkin LJ – but be irrefutable social information and data.

In this way the courts can demonstrate, as some judges have already tried to do, that property is not extrinsic to concerns of basic human liberty in today's increasingly 'rights-conscious' society. They can show that when we pose questions of liberty, such as the liberty to own property, we must pose them equally in relation to the weak as to the strong, because of the equal moral worth of all individuals that contemporary citizenship concerns demand. They can consistently demonstrate that laws respecting property must be staked out on morally defensible grounds, otherwise one could have the kind of decision – such as that of Lord Wilberforce, overruling the Court of Appeal, in *Midland Bank* v. *Green* – that gives property a decidedly immoral basis in society. But perhaps most importantly they can speak truth to power. They can use the adjudicative process to reject the idea of law as an end in itself, and underline that its power should be treated as a medium of outreach for vulnerable and underserved populations in an area of social activity too often controlled by large corporations and powerful individuals. These propositions, if embraced, would comprise part of a new jurisprudence that conceives of all law – through a concern for citizenship rights for all – as a manifestation of something beyond itself; a witness to something greater, to a collective fulfilment of a higher aspiration to a more meaningful and secure future for all society's members, and to a more contended communal existence.

Select Bibliography

Books

Anderson, J. Stuart (1992) *Lawyers and the Making of English Land Law 1832–1940*. London.
Arendt, Hannah (1961) *Between Past and Future*. London.
Baker, John H. (1990) *An Introduction to Legal History*. London.
Bentham, Jeremy (1859) *Principles of the Civil Code of Property* (ed. Bowring). London.
Bickel, Alexander (1962) *The Least Dangerous Branch: The Supreme Court at the Bar of Politics*. Indianapolis.
Bickel, Alexander (1970) *The Supreme Court and the Idea of Progress*. New York.
Clarke, Simon (1982) *Marx, Marginalism and Modern Sociology*. London.
Cole, G. D. H. and Postgate, R. (1946) *The Common People*. London.
Friedman, Milton (1962) *Capitalism and Freedom*. Chicago.
Hackney, Jeffery (1987) *Understanding Equity and Trusts*. London.
Harris, J. W. (1996) *Property and Justice*. Oxford.
Juss, Satvinder (1997) *Discretion and Deviation in the Administration of Immigration Control*. London.
Laski, Harold (1934) *A Grammar of Politics* (3rd edn). London.
Locke, John (1967) *Two Treatises of Government*. Cambridge.
Marshall, T. H. (1950) *Citizenship and Social Class*. Cambridge.
Miliband, Ralph (1984) *Capitalist Democracy in Britain*. Oxford.
Murphy, W. T. and Roberts, Simon (1987) *Understanding Property Law*. London.
Nozick, Robert (1974) *Anarchy, State and Utopia*. Oxford.
Offer, Avner (1981) *Property and Politics 1870–1914*. Oxford.
Pollock and Maitland, J. W. (1968 edn) *The History of English Law*. London.
Rawls, John (1971) *A Theory of Justice*. Oxford.
Savage, David (1992) *Turning Right: The Making of the Rehnquist Supreme Court*. New York.
Strum, Philippa (1995) *Brandeis on Democracy*. Kansas.
Tawney, R. A. (1924) *The Acquisitive Society*. London.
Thompson, E. P. (1975) *England in the Nineteenth Century*. London.
Thompson, E. P. (1990) *Whigs and Hunters*. London.
Wolin, Sheldon (1961) *Politics and Vision*. Boston.

Articles

Baxi, Upendra (1993) Judicial discourse: the dialectics of the face and the mask. *Journal of the Indian Law Institute.*

Boseley, Sarah (1995) Going cheap: the repossessed stuff of broken dreams. *Guardian*, 2 June.

Bright, Steven (1991) Beyond sham and into pretence. *Oxford Journal of Legal Studies* (11), p. 136.

Fehlberg, Belinda (1994) The husband, the bank, the wife and her signature. *Modern Law Review.*

Honore, A. M. (1987) Ownership. *Oxford Essays in Jurisprudence.*

Juss, Satvinder (1996) Human rights and the adversarial interest in contracts: a case study of good faith in property transactions. *Essays in European Law and Israel* (ed. A. M. Rabello), pp. 769–80. Jerusalem.

Moorhouse, H. F. (1973) The political incorporation of the British working class. *Sociology* (7), 3.

Offer, Avner (1977) The origin of the Law of Property Acts 1910–1925. *Modern Legal Studies* (40), p. 505.

Reich, Charles (1964) The new property. *Yale Law Journal.*

Thompson, Michael P. (1995) A very wide discretion? *The Conveyancer.*

Index

INDEX